AF575394

TITIAN'S
MAN IN A RED HAT

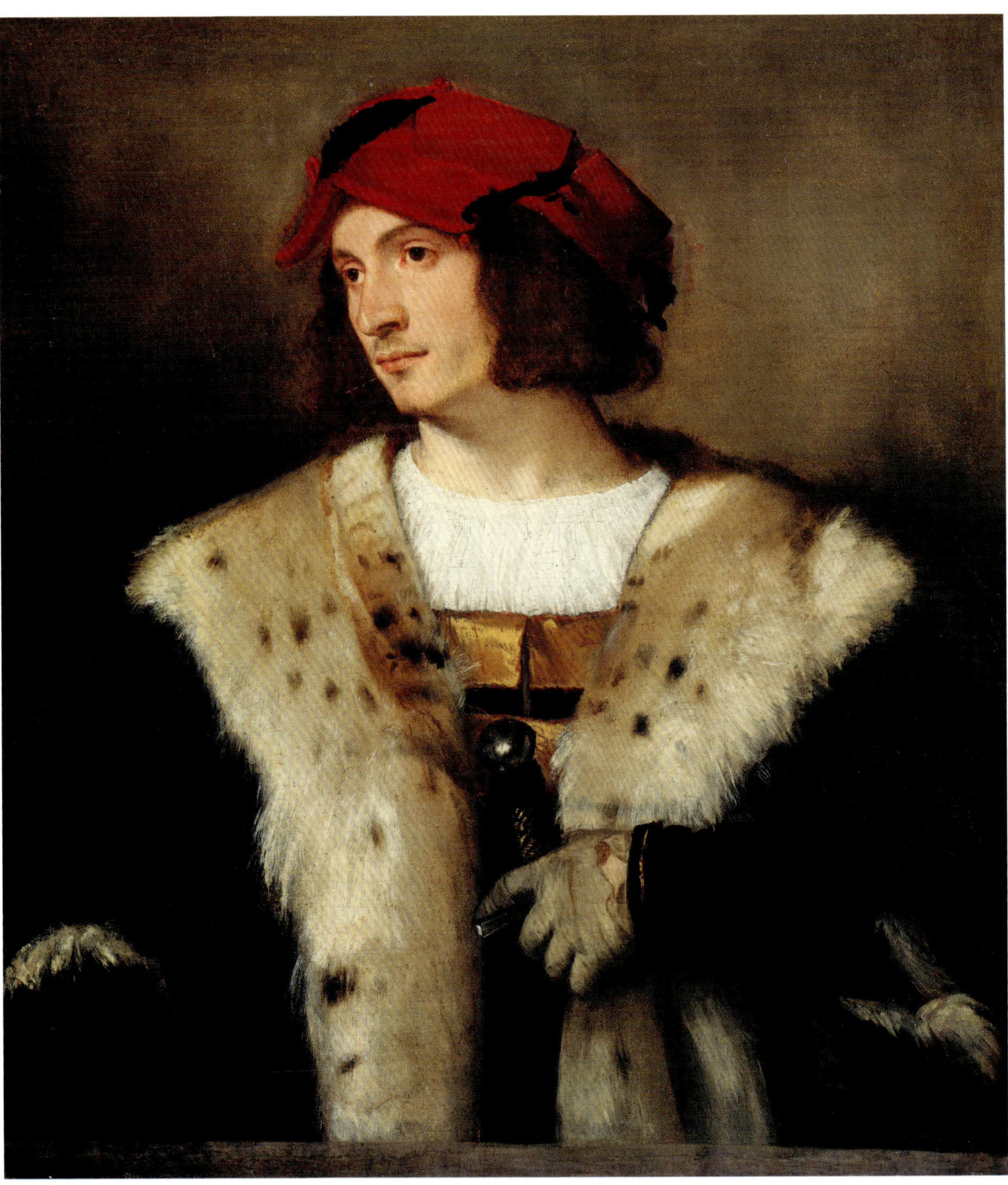

TITIAN'S MAN IN A RED HAT

Giulio Dalvit

Elizabeth Peyton

The Frick Collection, New York
in association with D Giles Limited

g

FRICK DIPTYCH SERIES

Designed to foster critical engagement and interest specialist and non-specialist alike, each book in this series illuminates a single work in the Frick's rich collection with an essay by a Frick curator paired with a contribution from a contemporary artist or writer.

First published in 2022 by The Frick Collection
1 East 70th Street
New York, NY 10021
www.frick.org

Michaelyn Mitchell, Editor in Chief
Christopher Snow Hopkins, Assistant Editor

In association with GILES
An imprint of D Giles Limited
66 High Street
Lewes, BN7 1XG, UK
gilesltd.com

Copyedited and proofread by Sarah Kane
Designed by Caroline and Roger Hillier,
The Old Chapel Graphic Design

Produced by GILES

Printed and bound in China

A CIP catalogue record for this book is available from the Library of Congress.

ISBN 978-1-913875-30-5

Pages 10–29 (**"The Friend" by Elizabeth Peyton**) are designed by Elizabeth Peyton with assistance from Jules Estèves, and the text preserves the author's original punctuation, grammar, and spacing.

Cover and page 30: details from Titian's *Portrait of a Man in a Red Hat* (frontispiece)
Frontispiece: Titian (Tiziano Vecellio), *Portrait of a Man in a Red Hat*, ca. 1516–19. Oil on canvas, 32¼ × 28 in. (81.9 × 71.1 cm). The Frick Collection, New York
Page 6: detail of Carlo Dolci (attributed to), *Portrait of a Young Man* (after Titian's *Portrait of a Man in a Red Hat*), n.d. (fig. 3)

CONTENTS

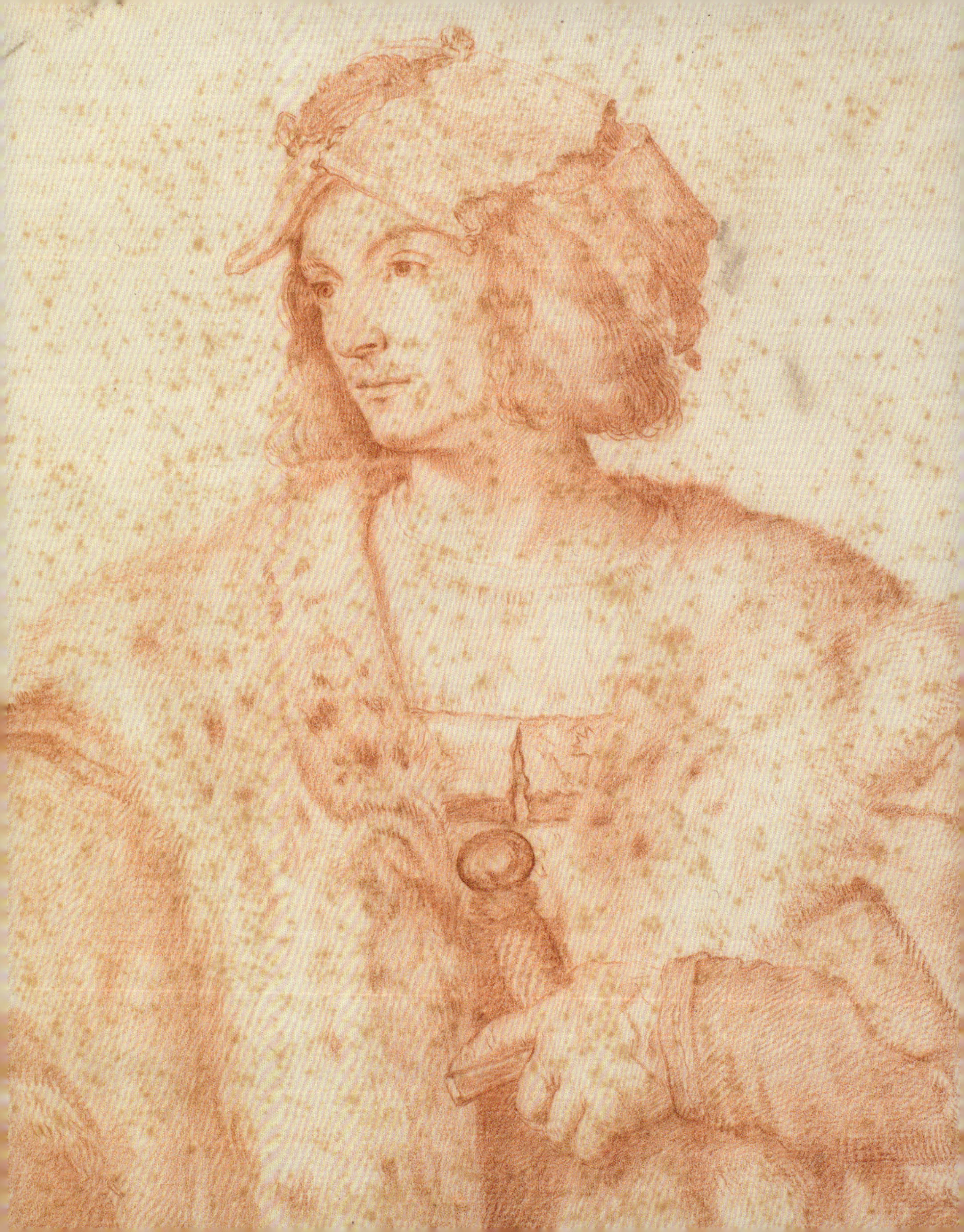

DIRECTOR'S FOREWORD

This tenth volume in the Frick's Diptych series considers one of the most enigmatic works in the Frick's collection. Virtually nothing is known for certain about Titian's *Portrait of a Man in a Red Hat*. Who is the sitter? We know from his velvet hat, lynx-lined garment, slashed gloves, and rapier that the dandyish subject was a man of consequence in Renaissance Venice. Titian perfectly captures not only the sitter's attire but also his *moti dell'animo* (vagaries of the spirit) and the modish melancholia of the moment. As the art historian John Shearman put it, "This Hamlet of the Lagoons seems rather self-indulgently to have chosen to be sicklied o'er with the pale cast of thought."

Giulio Dalvit, the Frick's Assistant Curator of Sculpture, addresses the mystery of this morose sitter with rigor and verve, deconstructing the allure of Titian's portrait and greatly enriching our knowledge of the painting. His essay is complemented by a selection of works by the celebrated artist Elizabeth Peyton that traces her engagement with Titian (and his fellow Venetian Giorgione) from 1986 to the present. We owe our sincere thanks to both contributors.

We extend our gratitude to Editor in Chief Michaelyn Mitchell, who expertly oversaw the production of the publication and, with Assistant Editor Christopher Snow Hopkins, revised the principal essay. We would also like to acknowledge our longtime publishing partner D Giles Limited.

Ian Wardropper
Anna-Maria and Stephen Kellen Director, The Frick Collection

ACKNOWLEDGMENTS

Over the months of research for, and the writing of, this book, I have benefited from the knowledge and support of many friends, mentors, and colleagues. I wish to thank, in particular, Maria Stella Alfonsi, Agostino Allegri, Christopher Apostle, Saida Bondini, Linda Borean, Emerson Bowyer, Jane Bridgeman, Fausto Calderai, Marcello Calogero, Adriana Concin, Kira d'Alburquerque, Paola Di Rico, Pasquale Focarile, Caitlin Henningsen, Virginia Hill, Leonard Horsch, Rebecca J. Long, Marco Magnifico, Emily Markham, Scott Nethersole, Morna O'Neill, Nicholas Penny, Federica Pich, Giovanni Renzi, Álvaro Romero Sanchez-Arjona, Patricia Rubin, Mario Scalini, Maddalena Taglioli, Mario Tavella, Pierre Terjanian, and Giulia Zaccariotto. I am also grateful to Gian Giacomo Attolico Trivulzio and Lord James Methuen-Campbell for their generosity in sharing with me their knowledge about their respective families and their collections.

At the Frick, Joseph Godla's analysis of Titian's painting led me to a better understanding of many aspects of its support, as well as the technique used. Many thanks go to Sally Brazil and Julie Ludwig for helping me to navigate the vastness of the museum's archives. Michaelyn Mitchell has, once again, worked her magic on the text and adeptly managed the production of the book. My thanks are also owed to Christopher Snow Hopkins for helping to edit the text and for introducing me to William Carlos Williams's inspiring words on the *Man in a Red Hat*. It is only due to the unremitting assistance of Ralph Baylor, Gemma McElroy, and Rebecca Leonard that I was able to obtain book scans and image files during a global pandemic. Eveline Baseggio Omiccioli, an intern at the Frick in 2009–10, must also be credited for assembling some bibliographic materials on the painting, which I was still able to consult many years later.

Were it not for Alessandro Nova, who kindly invited me to spend several months as a Visiting Fellow at the Kunsthistorisches Institut in Florence, this book would have never seen the light of day. Funnily enough, it was in an apartment on Via Ghibellina, right across the street from Palazzo Borghese—formerly Palazzo Salviati, where the Titian painting might have spent some time—that I wrote away my Florentine months.

Xavier F. Salomon, to whom I am ineffably thankful, followed this project and encouraged me every step of the way. It is certainly to Elizabeth Peyton that I owe the greatest debt of gratitude for this book. She and I shared a memorable trip together to Pieve di Cadore, and she has since taught me a new way to connect to portraits and painters.

These pages are dedicated to G.I., C.P., G.P., and F.Z., "cari e certi e veri amici."

Giulio Dalvit
Assistant Curator of Sculpture, The Frick Collection

THE FRIEND

by Elizabeth Peyton

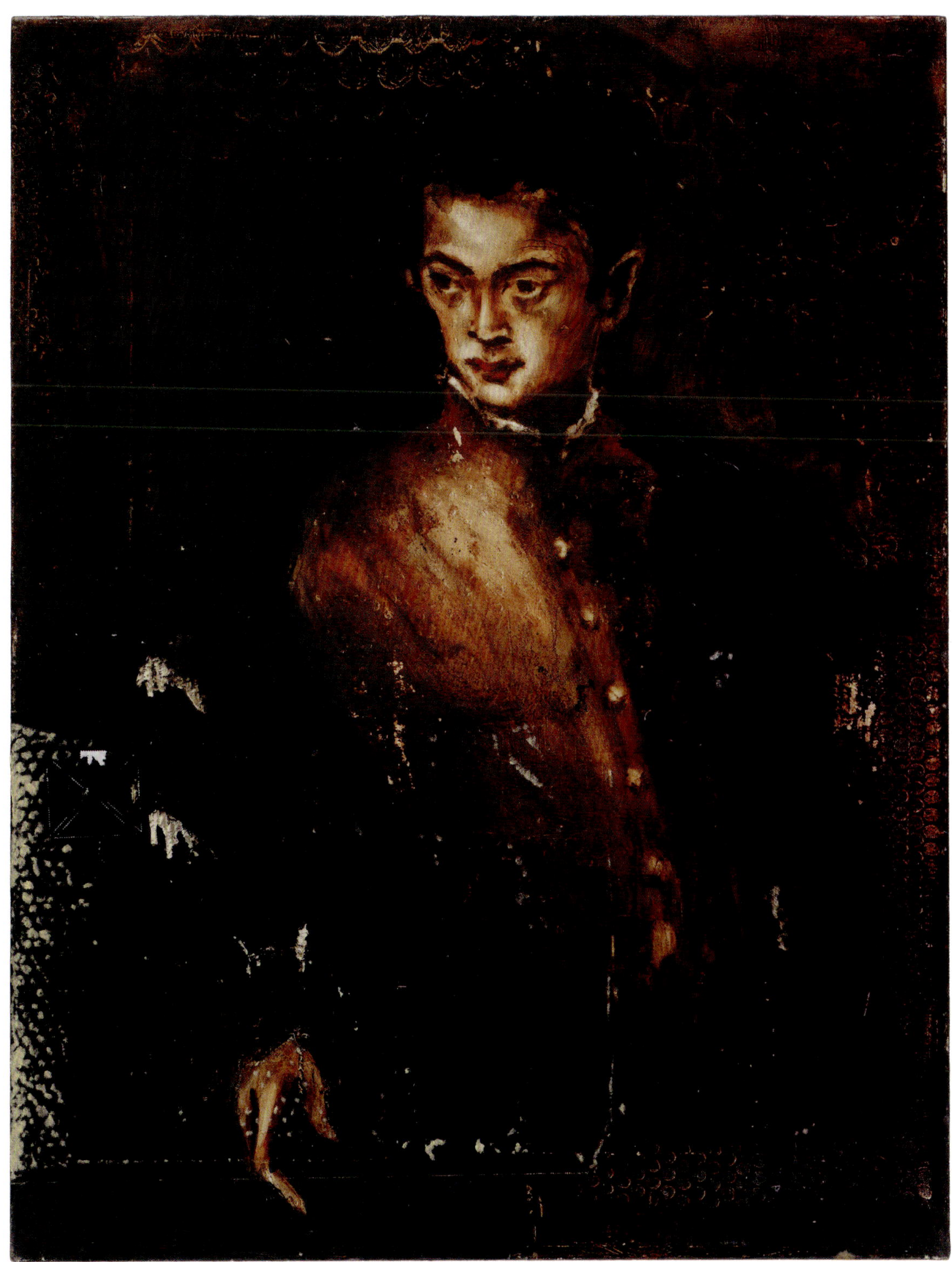

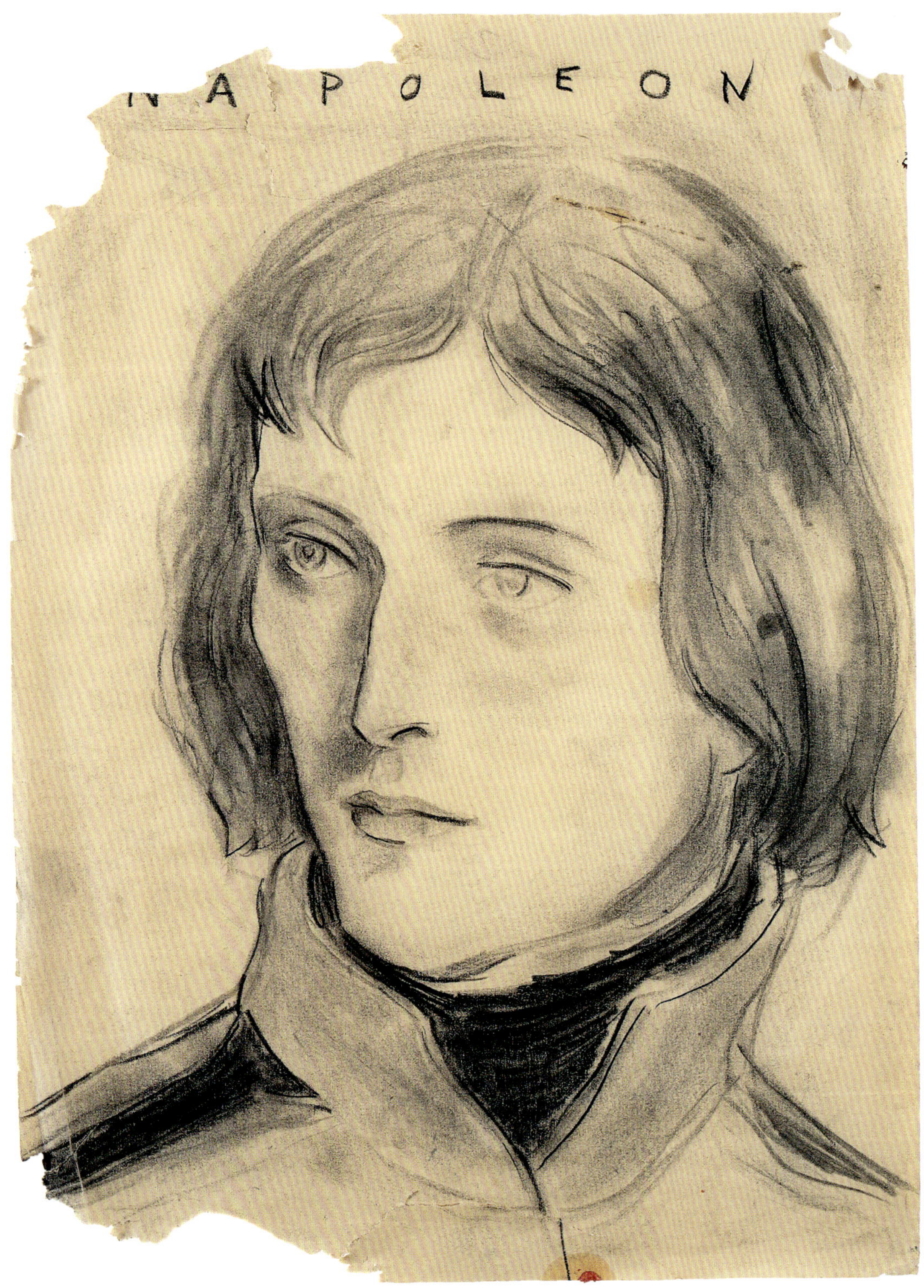
NAPOLEON

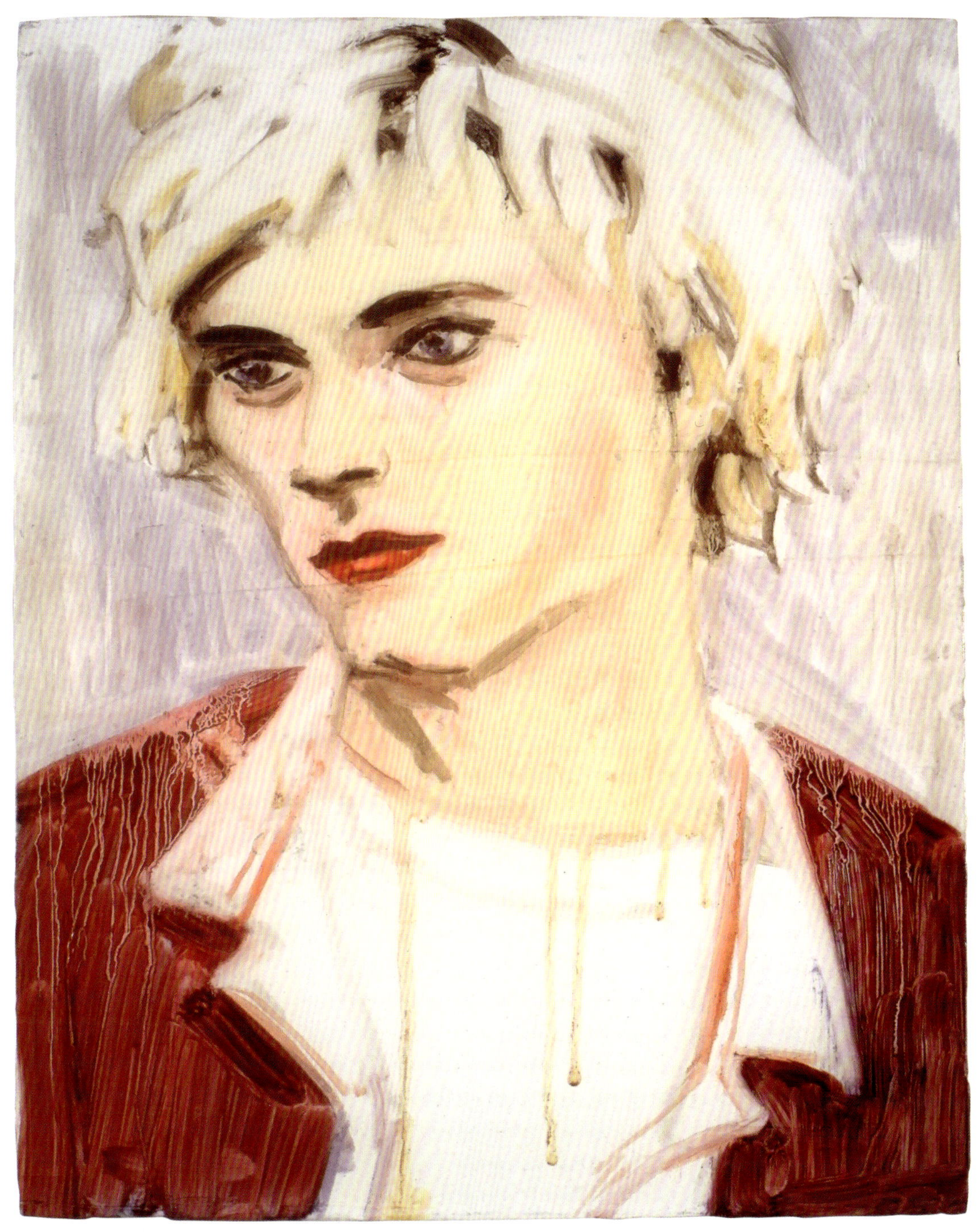

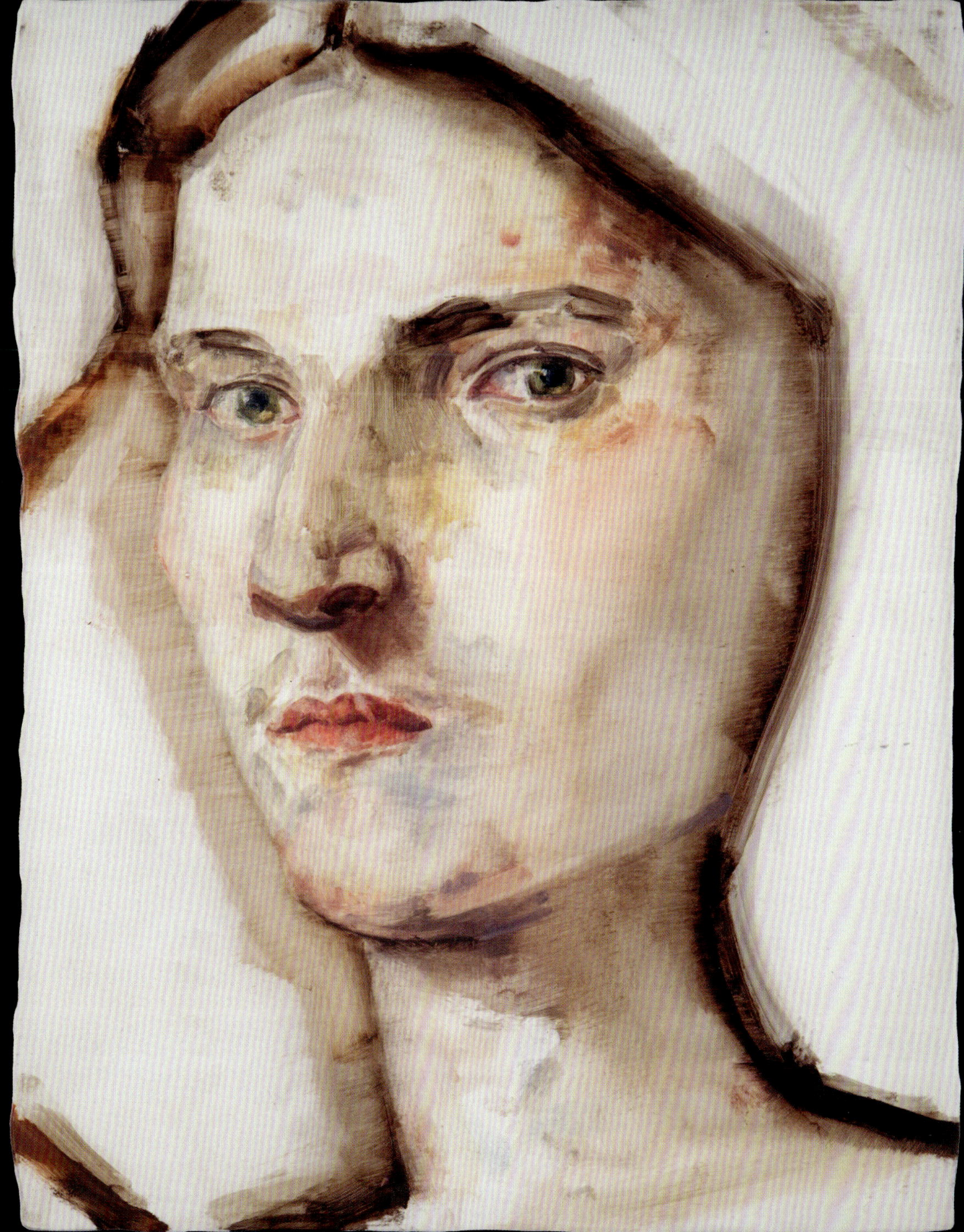

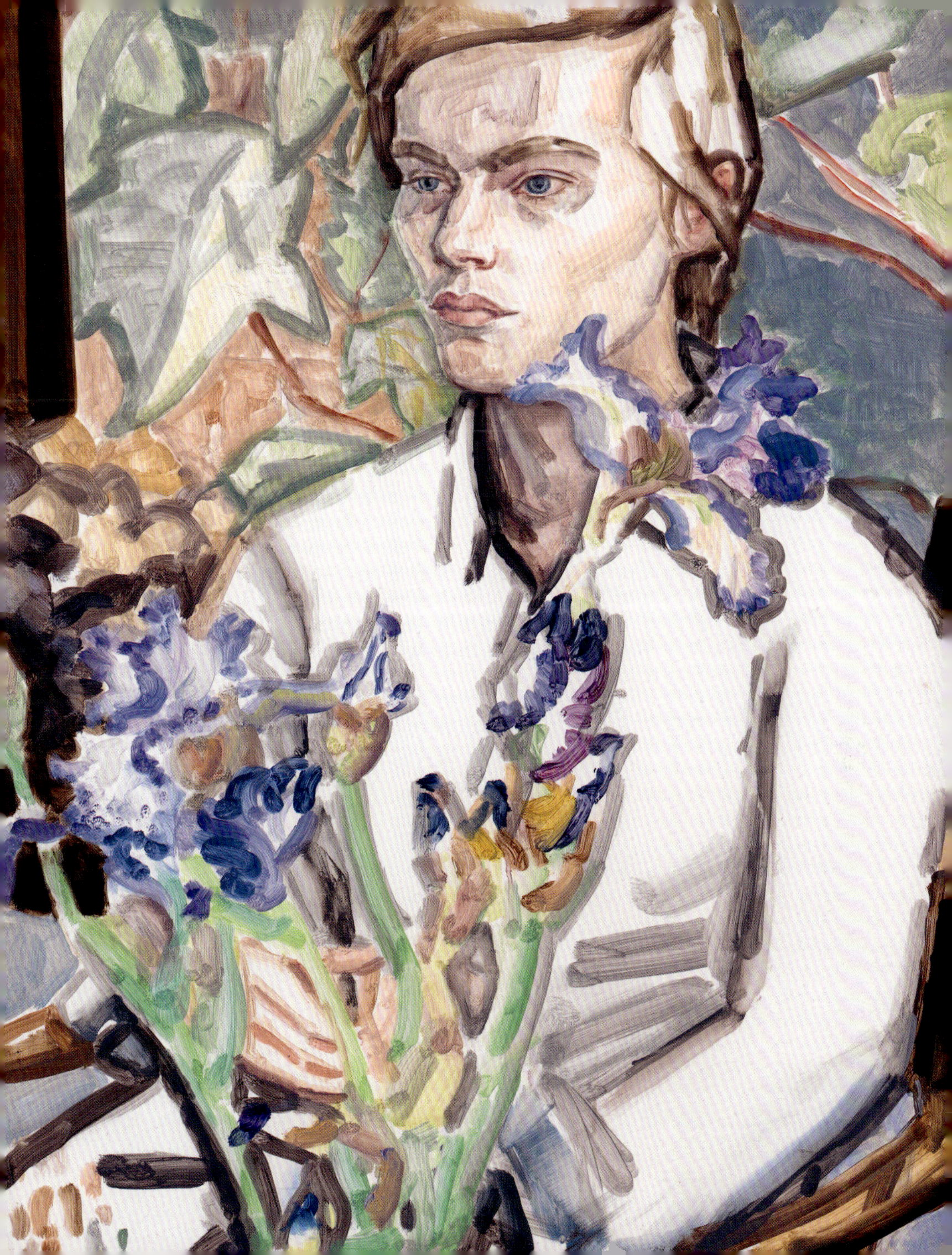

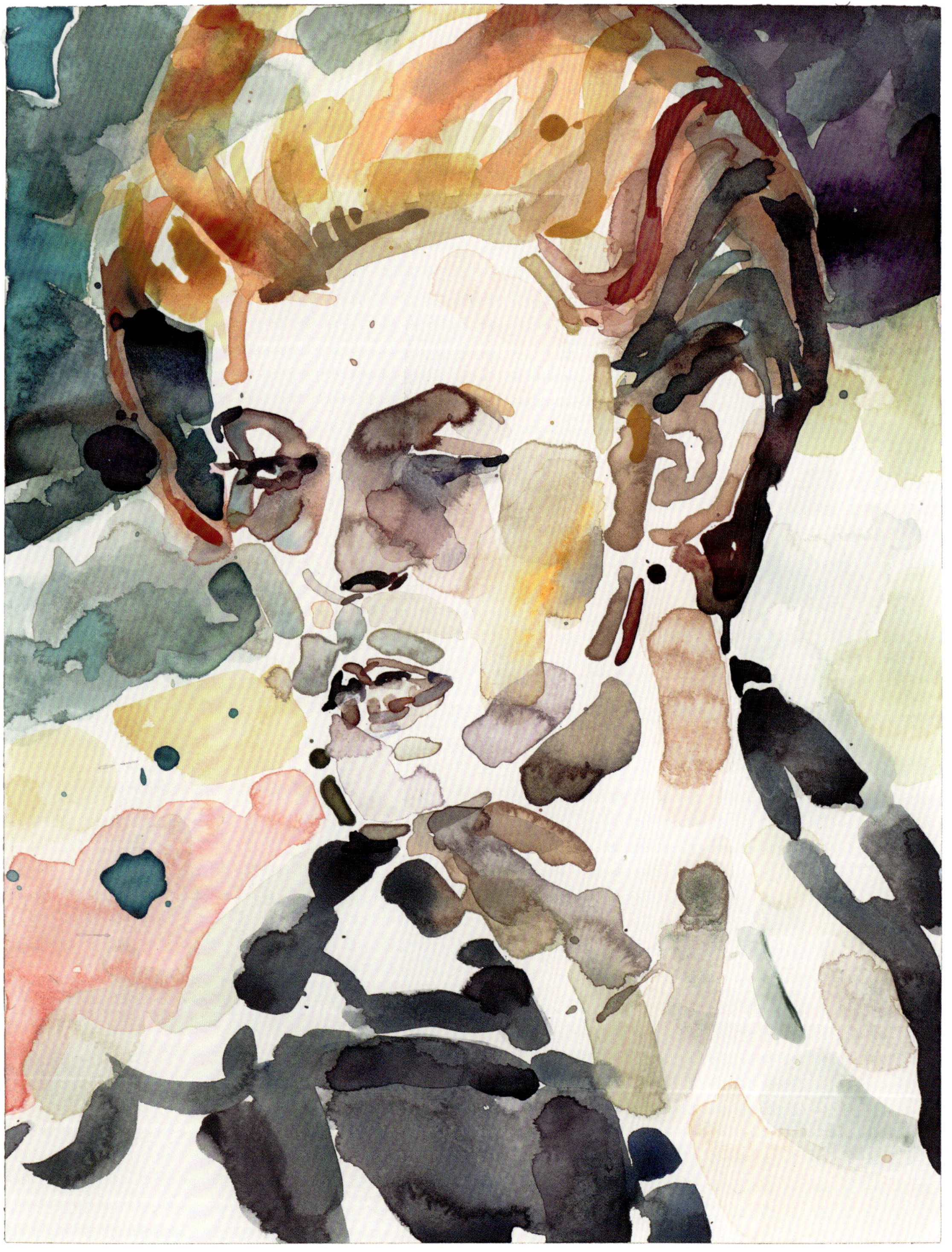

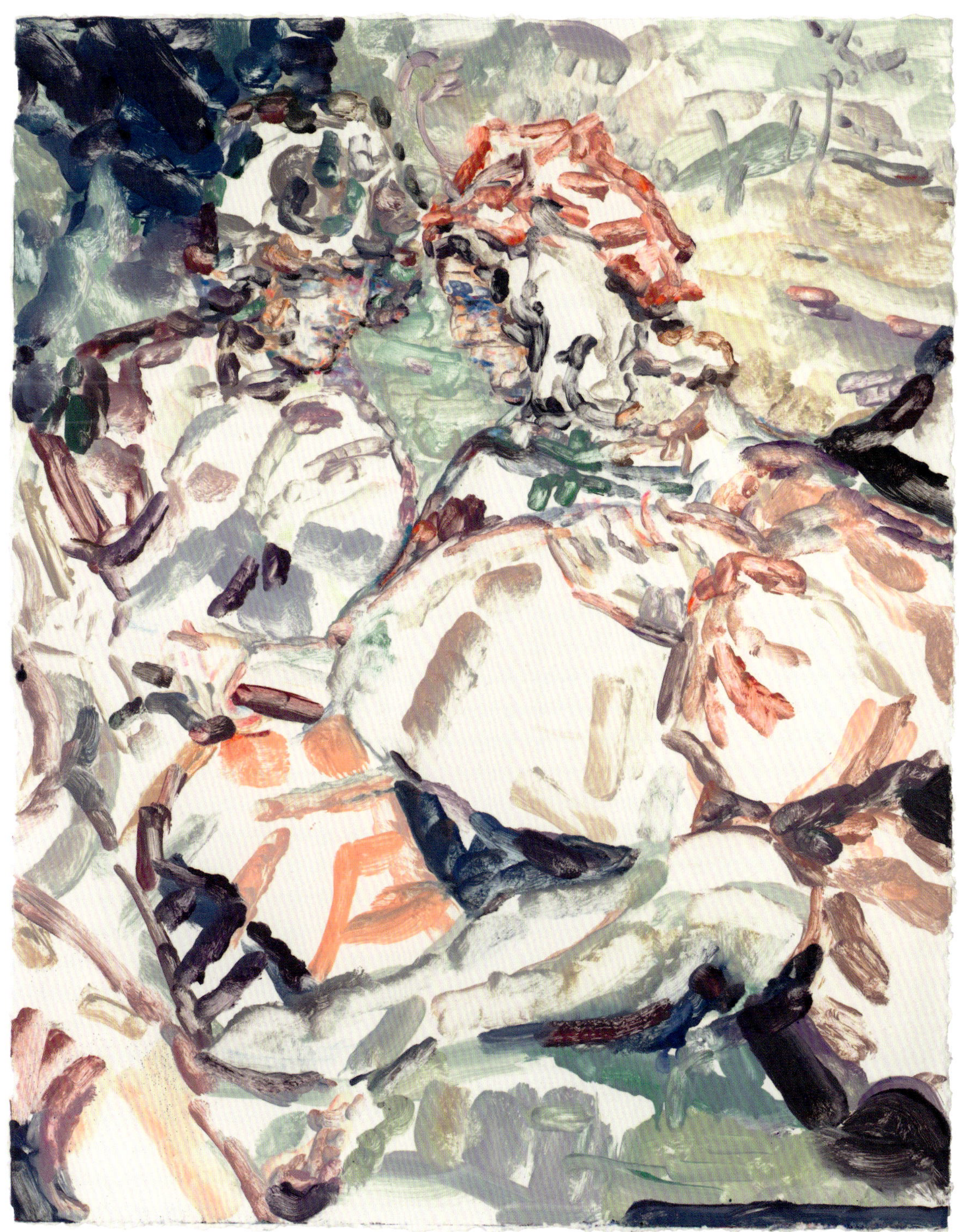

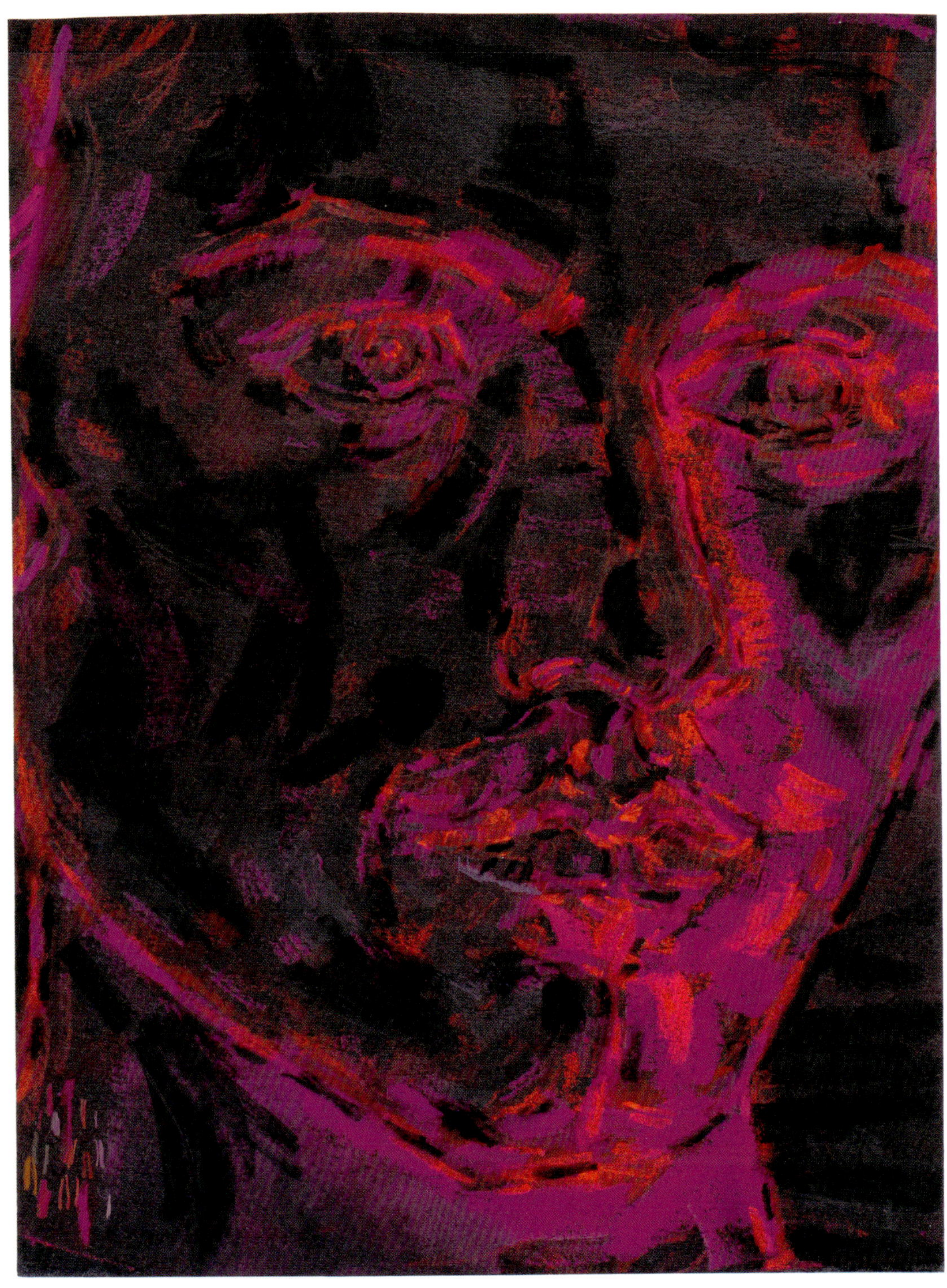

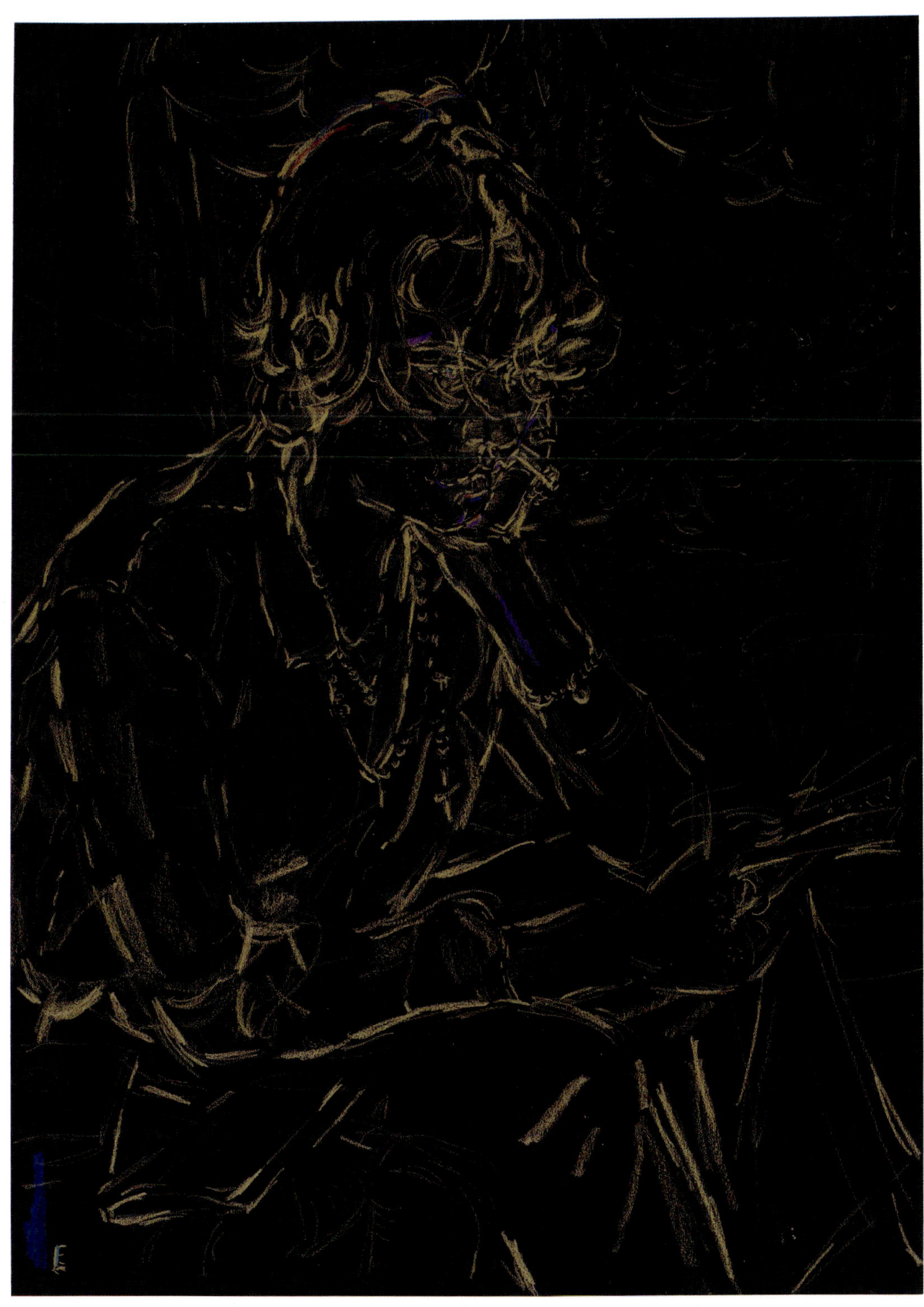

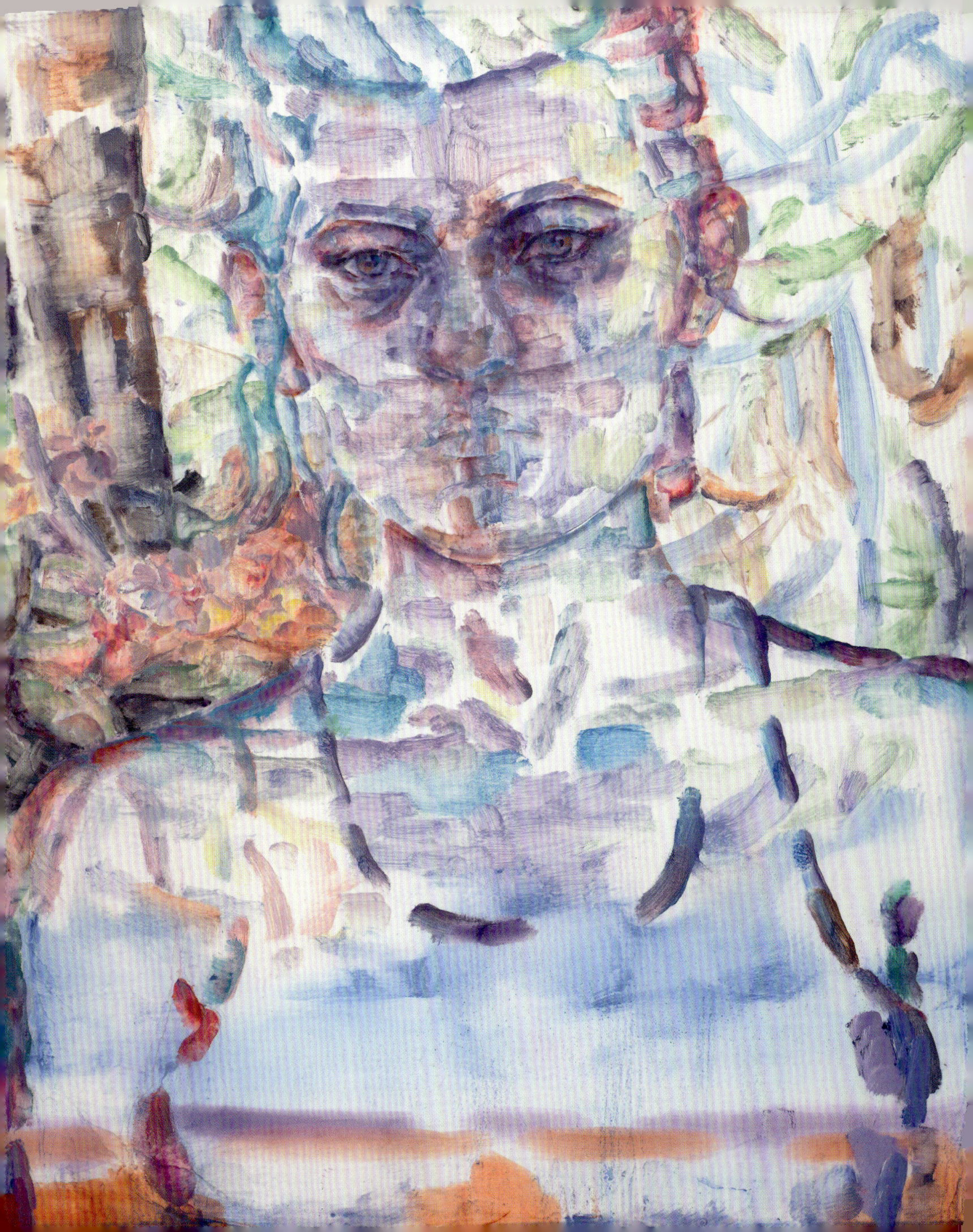

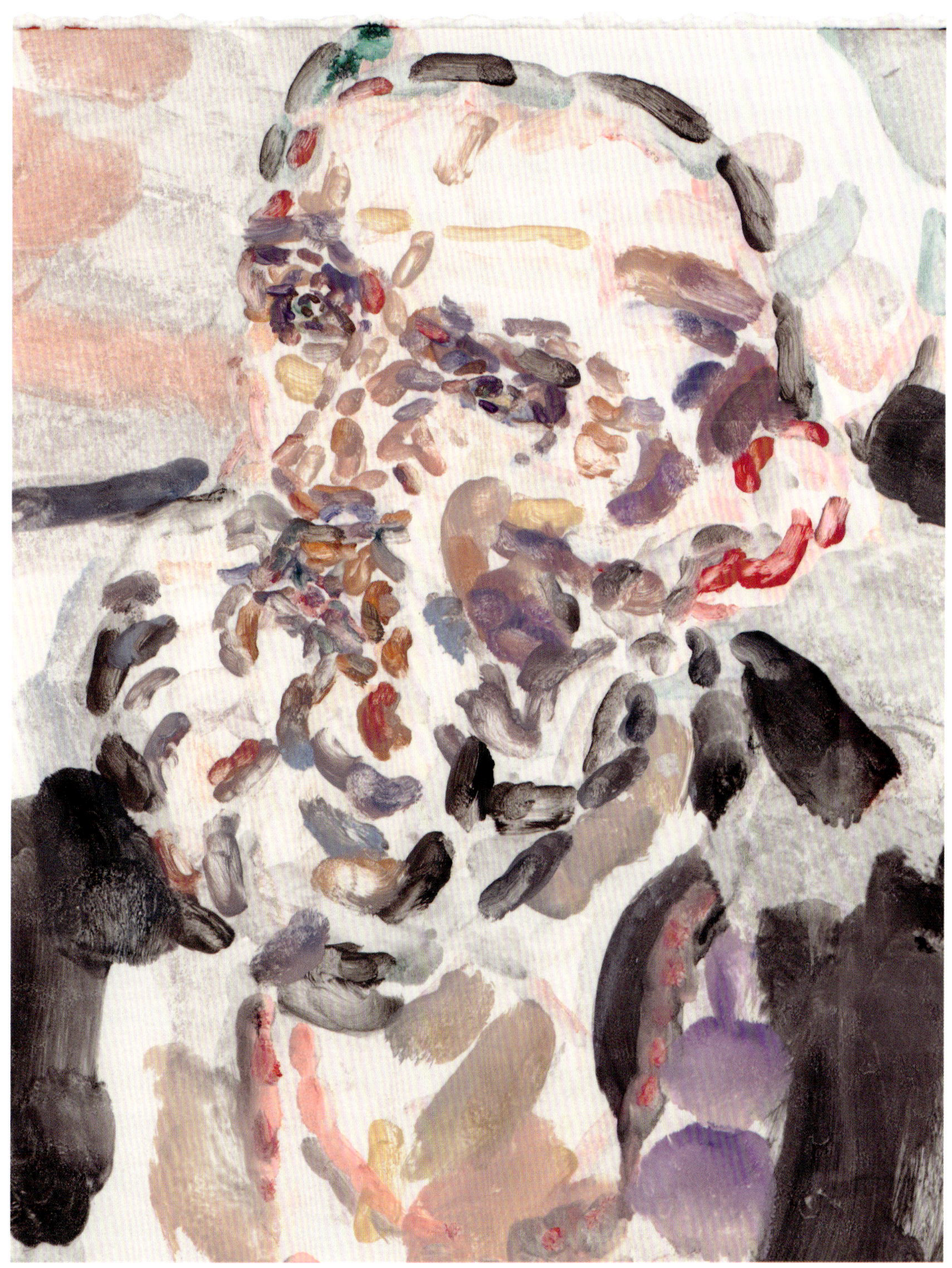

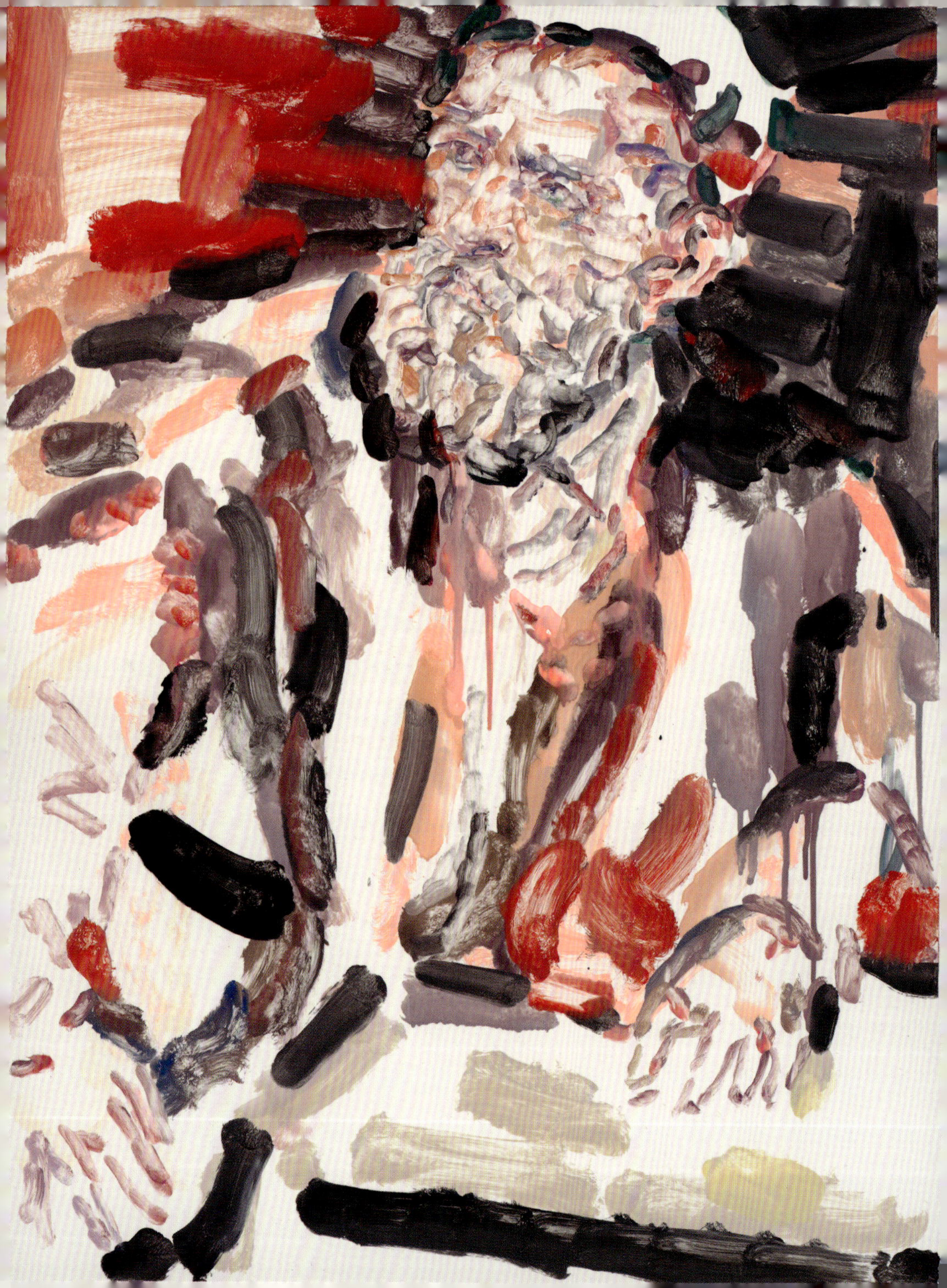

The Friend

Elizabeth Peyton, New York City, 2021

In the 10th grade of Brookfield High School our English teacher, Mr Altschuler, broke the news to us "There is No beauty without Sadness"... I begged to differ and
determinedly set out to prove him wrong... but could find no example ...... One of the first stops on the path to understanding
must have been my first visit to the The Frick Collection in 1983 and especially to set eyes on Titian's *Portrait of a Man in a Red Hat*... I think I was around the same age as the subject of that painting, 18,
some years younger than Titian was when he painted it... Newly moved to New York City, attending the School of Visual Arts... I was mesmerized by this picture... and then to now I'm still expanding my feelings about this picture, that face, this painter...

Soon after I did make a "copy" of this picture (I can't show you!!) and also the one included here of after Titian's painting of Ranuccio Farnese. Titian is a teacher, wonder and inspiration for me in every way, which led me to making these recent portraits of him...
"Who are you tattered fur wearing, red beaded, bearded dynamo artist from Pieve di Cadore?" ...... How did you capture the universe in flesh?

I know the feeling and literally the composition of *Portrait of a Man in a Red Hat* is a seed that's been growing in my work since I first saw it and my intention to make something specific but eternal is within all of these pictures.

Recently I made another work after a Titian painting—*Man with a Glove* —I concentrated on the face—and came to understand that in the midst of winter 2021 (Pandemic time) I was yearning for the compassion in that face— for a friend whose face I could rest on.

All works on pp. 11–29
by Elizabeth Peyton

Page 11
After Titian (Ranuccio Farnese, 1542), 1986
Oil on linen
40⅛ × 30 in.
(101.9 × 76.2 cm)

Page 12
Napoleon, 1991
Charcoal on paper
22 × 18 in.
(55.9 × 45.7 cm)

Page 13
Zoe's Kurt,1995
Oil on board
14 × 11 in.
(35.6 × 27.9 cm)

Page 15
After Giorgione, 2011
Oil on board
9⅛ × 12¼ in.
(23.2 × 31.1 cm)

Page 17
Irises and Klara Commerce St., 2012
Oil on panel
24 × 18 in. (61 × 45.7 cm)

Page 18
David, March 2017, 2017
Watercolor on paper
16 × 12 in.
(40.6 × 30.5 cm)

How is it a painter can make a portrait of an eighteen year old in a red hat and in it create a vehicle to speak about the whole arc of life and death? While he is breaking the news to you how fleeting this moment is, he is also tenderly making a place for you to be comforted: follow the descent of coloring in *Portrait of a Man in a Red Hat*'s cheek and you will get caught in pink descending to lilac, to gray, to blue, to linen and fur around to hands and metal, and golden mantles… His heavy lids holding some sorrow while the upturned shadow of his lips convey—it's ok— it will be all right… The beauty is the cause and cure for the sadness it evokes.

Around this time I was also yearning for the comforting friendship held in Titian's *Pastoral Concert*. I included a monotype I made after a detail of this work also in the winter of 2021 …… I like to imagine that it is a picture of Giorgione playing the lute to Titian as Giorgione died from the plague shortly before this painting was made. It isn't so much for the literal—bodies together—eyes between them—but the overall rhythm of the forms—that keeps you moving… the communion… it is painting not as a way to freeze frame life but to hold its energy and keep it moving in a two dimensional space that is ever alive!

Page 19
The Friends (after Titian's Pastoral Concert 1509), 2021
Monotype, pastel and pencil on Twinrocker handmade paper
26½ × 20½ in.
(67.3 × 52.1 cm)

Page 20
The Friend, 2021
Pastel and colored pencil on black paper
$7\tfrac{15}{16} \times 5\tfrac{13}{16}$ in.
(20.2 × 14.8 cm)

Page 21
Elias, July 2021, 2021
Color pencil on black paper
$11\tfrac{11}{16} \times 8\tfrac{17}{64}$ in.
(29.7 × 21 cm)

Page 23
Elizabeth, 2021
Oil on board
14 × 11 in.
(35.6 × 27.9 cm)

Page 25
Titian (After Titian) #2, 2021
Monotype on Twinrocker handmade paper
43½ × 31½ in.
(110.5 × 80 cm)

Page 26
Titian (After Titian) #1, 2021
Monotype on Twinrocker handmade paper
43½ × 31½ in.
(110.5 × 80 cm)

Page 29
After Titian's Man with the Red Hat, 2021
Watercolor on Paper
24 × 18 in. (61 × 45.7 cm)

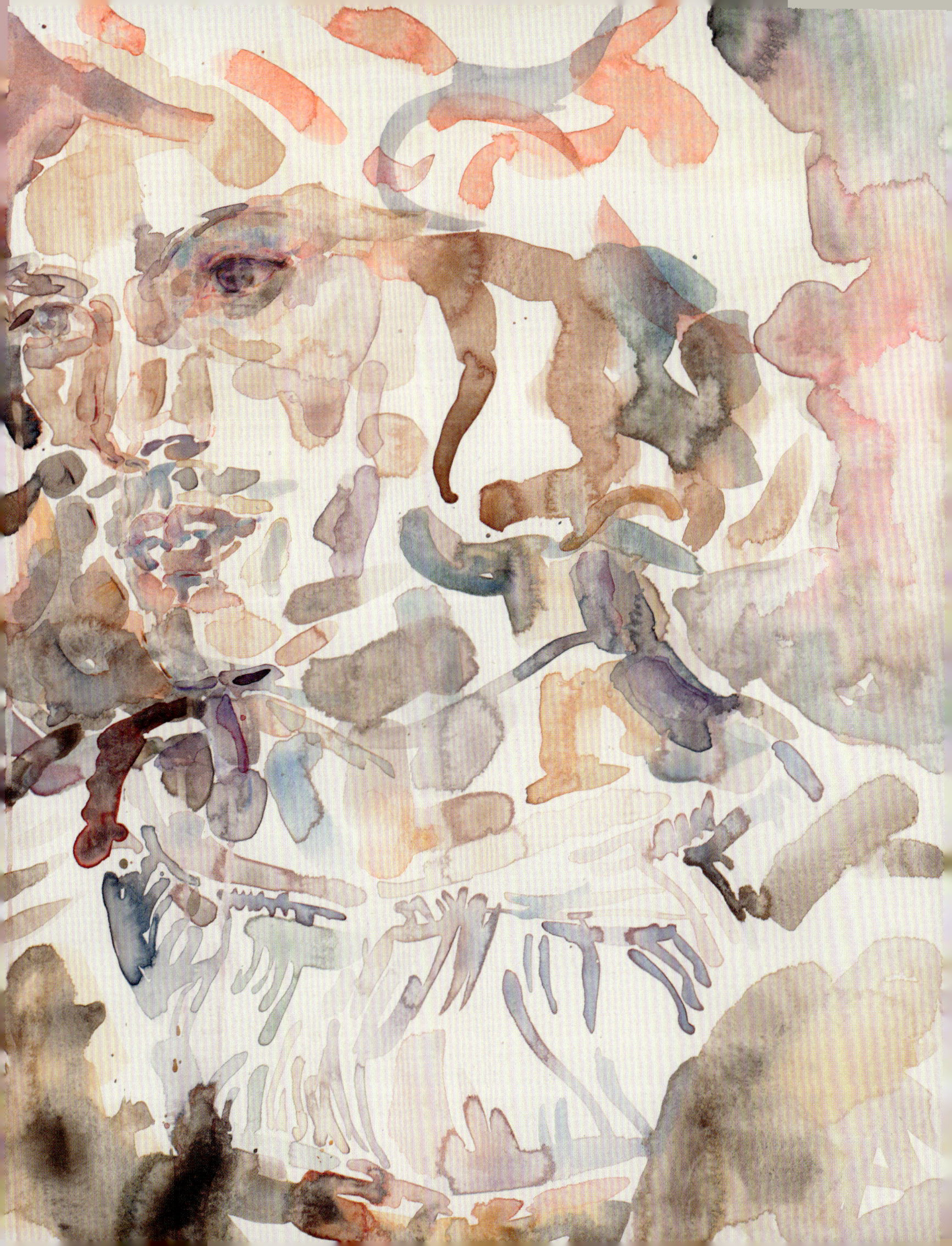

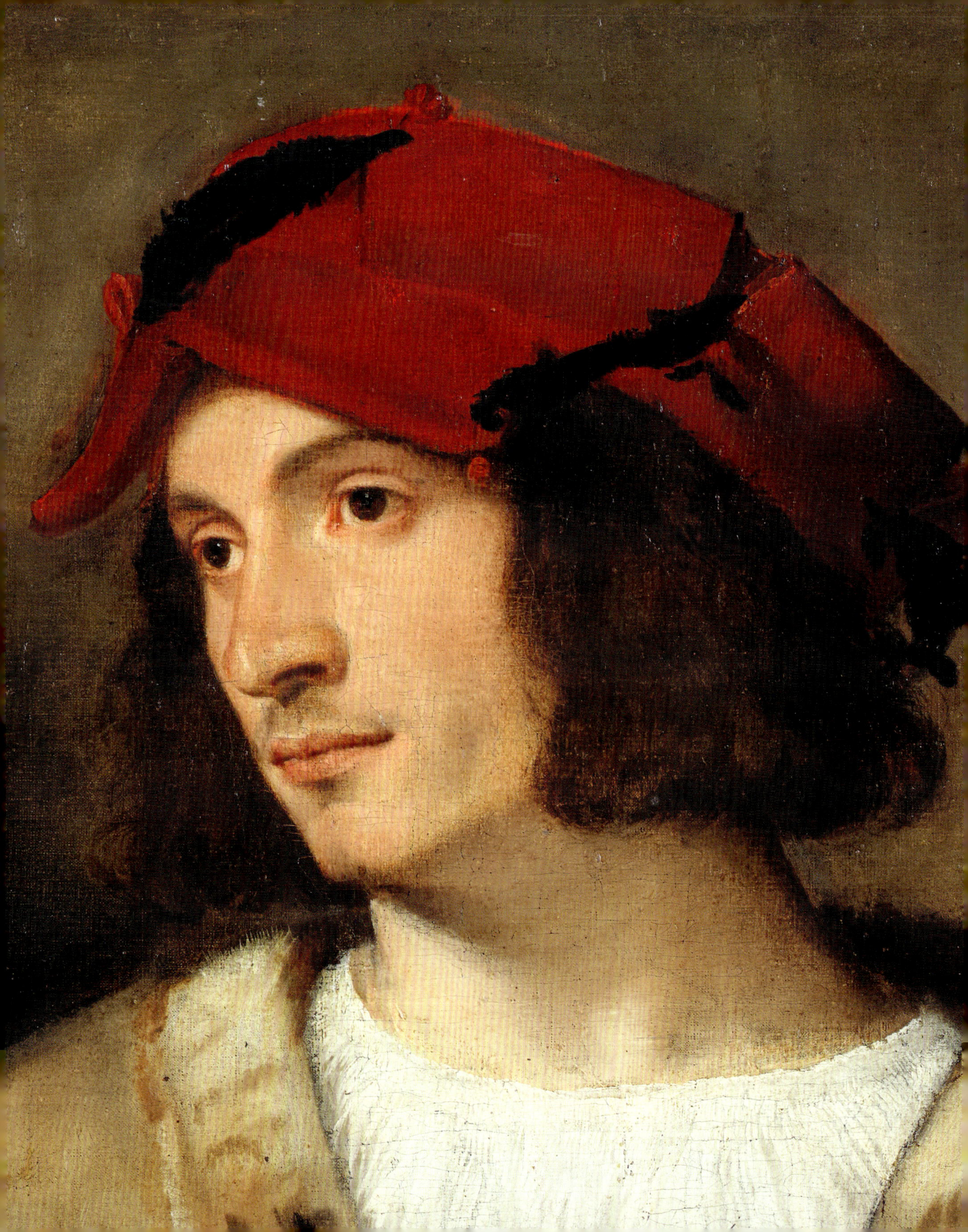

TITIAN'S PORTRAIT OF A MAN IN A RED HAT

Giulio Dalvit

Titian's *Portrait of a Man in a Red Hat* was featured on the cover of *Life* magazine in August of 1947 (fig. 1), and in 1962 it appeared in one of Donald Judd's terse *Writings*, to name but two of the painting's many cameos outside The Frick Collection, where it has been on display for more than a century.[1] Of its many viewer reactions, possibly the most poignant is that on the back of a postcard of the painting sent by William Carlos Williams to his friend, the poet Louis Zukofsky. Dated February 21, 1952, the card reads: "This, at the Frick Museum, is for all time: annihilates time as far as poor mortals may."[2] Collapsing the difference between portrait ("this") and sitter ("poor mortal"), Williams's comment captures one of the portrait's salient qualities—its ability to conjure a human presence before one's eyes, to make us forget both the portrait's thingness and the world we live in.

Arresting and beloved as Titian's portrait may be, virtually nothing is known about it. Its dating is far from firmly established, its sitter remains unidentified, its attribution has been intermittently questioned, and its provenance has been the subject of much debate. On May 14, 1906, soon after an auction sale in London that included Titian's portrait, a journalist for *The Times* of London wrote:

> By far the most important among the miscellaneous properties was a much-discussed good North Italian portrait of a comparatively young man to three-quarter length, standing, directed to front and looking to left, in dark cloak

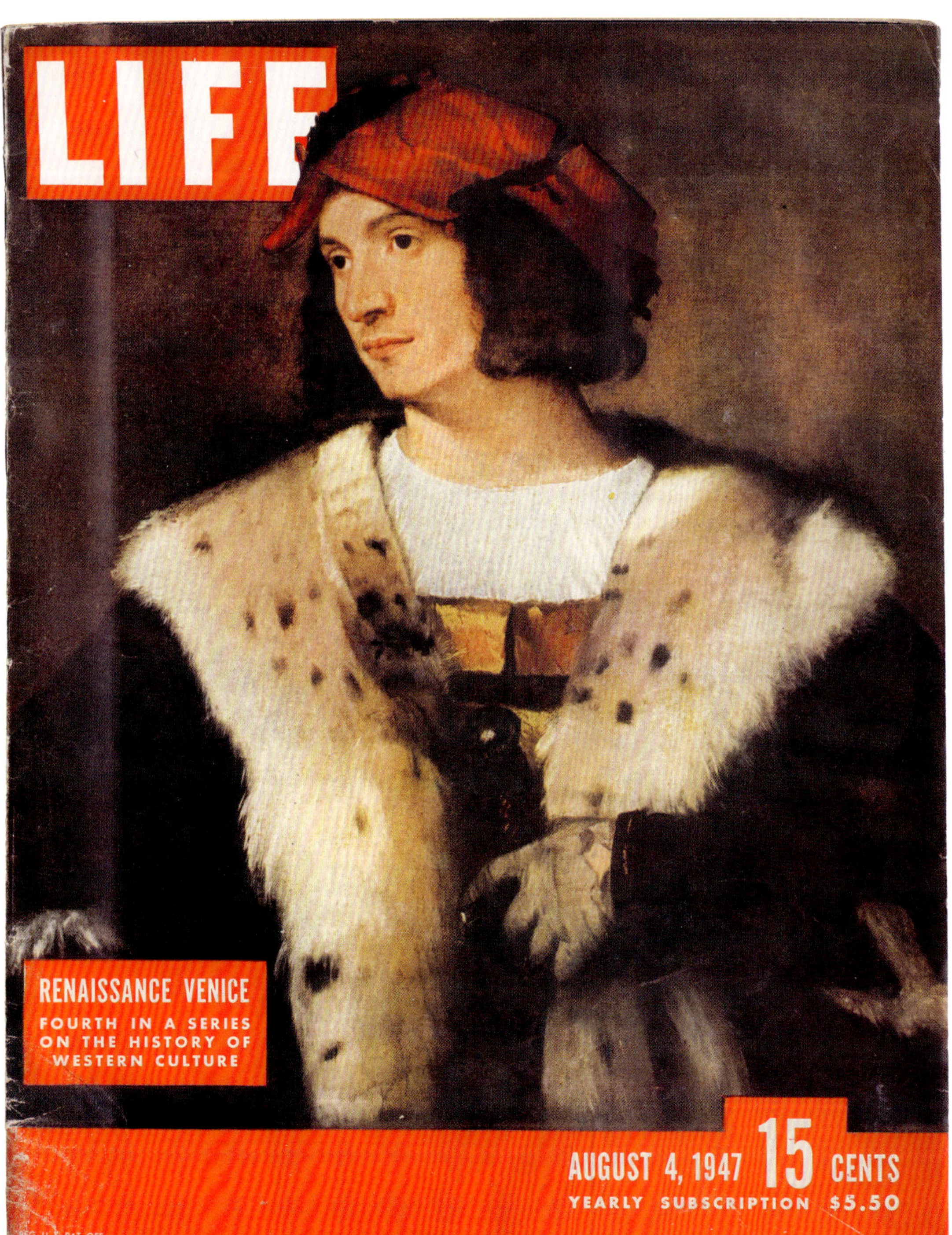
LIFE
RENAISSANCE VENICE
FOURTH IN A SERIES
ON THE HISTORY OF
WESTERN CULTURE
AUGUST 4, 1947
15 CENTS
YEARLY SUBSCRIPTION $5.50
REG. U.S. PAT. OFF.

> trimmed with grey fur, and red cap and long hair, holding a dagger or sword by the hilt, on canvas, 30 ½ in. by 25 ½ in.; it is catalogued as by Titian and as representing Lorenzo di Medici, but it is not by Titian, neither does it represent Lorenzo di Medici (unless Lorenzo II [i.e., Lorenzo, Duke of Urbino] is intended). Various artists have been suggested as having painted this portrait, notably Sebastian del Piombo, Lotto, and Cariani. It was started at 20 guineas, and at 2,100 guineas it fell to Mr. [Hugh] Lane. This is one of the most remarkable picture "bargains" of the season, as the picture was purchased at Christie's in 1876 for the small sum of 91 guineas by a "Mr. Waters." It was then described as "from Foots Cray Place," which, it may be mentioned, was a famous residence built in the 18th century after a design by Palladio for Bou[r]chier Cleeve, "a pewterer of Cheapside."[3]

Fig. 1
Cover of *Life* magazine, August 4, 1947
Frick Art Reference Library, New York

Over the years, *The Times* closely followed the movements of the painting.[4] In 1914, the name of a member of the Methuen family—whose seat was, and is, Corsham Court in Wiltshire—was mentioned for the first time in relation to the provenance of the portrait now at the Frick:

> The much-discussed Titian portrait of a man with a red cap, which was brought from Italy in 1773 by Mr. Methuen, and was bought at 91 guineas at Christie's in 1876, was bought by Sir Hugh Lane in 1906 for 2,100 guineas. . . . Yesterday bidding was started at 2,000 guineas and it returned to Sir Hugh Lane at 13,000 guineas, with Messrs. Colnaghi and Messrs. Agnew as the underbidders.[5]

The words of this anonymous reviewer for *The Times* must have caused a stir, as *The Times* reported on July 8, 1914:

> Lord Methuen [Paul S. Methuen, 3rd Baron Methuen] writes to say that the Titian portrait of a man in a red cap, recently the property of Mr. A[rthur] M[orton] Grenfell, was never in the Corsham collection made by Sir Paul Methuen in the early part of the 18th century.[6]

The journalist replied the following day, further substantiating his findings and revealing his name:

> Sir,
>
> as Lord Methuen writes to you that the Titian "Portrait of a Man with a Red Cap," recently the property of Mr. A. M. Grenfell, was "never in the Corsham collection made by Sir Paul Methuen in the early part of the 18th century" and many people still seem to be in doubt as to the *provenance* of

Fig. 2
Carlo Dolci
St. Andrew Praying before His Martyrdom, 1643
Oil on canvas
45½ × 36 in. (115.6 × 91.4 cm)
Birmingham Museum and Art Gallery, Birmingham

> the picture—so far, at least, as it can be verified—you will perhaps allow me to go into the matter shortly.
>
> There can be little doubt that this picture, together with some of the Methuen diamonds, was in the possession of Gratiana, daughter of one of the numerous members of the Methuen family who received the name of Paul. The Paul Methuen I have in mind lived about 1670, and married Sarah Gould. Gratiana was their daughter and married Rev. J. Rogers: they had a son, John Methuen, and a daughter, Elizabeth, who became the wife of Captain Wilson. Captain Wilson's daughter Elizabeth was adopted by her uncle, the John Methuen Rogers just mentioned, and in time married Rev. E[dward] Edgell, Prebendary of Wells, who died April 2, 1860. At his death the picture lately sold passed to his eldest son, who sent it to Christie's and bought it in at 91 guineas, on June 24 (not May 2), 1876.
>
> I may add that the information which I have got together during the last two or three years is in part derived from the "Pedigree of the Methuen Family," by W.H. Jones and J. Beddoe, while the correspondence and interviews which I have had with the descendants of the collateral branch of the Methuen of Corsham family who owned the picture down to 1906 affords confirmation. The other facts are now common knowledge.
>
> I am, Sir, yours truly,
> Maurice W. Brockwell[7]

The next month, in the "Sale Room" section of *The Connoisseur*, the history of Titian's *Man in a Red Hat* was articulated further:

> This work has a comparatively brief but eventful history. Mr. Maurice Brockwell has traced its possession to Gratiana, daughter of Paul Methuen—not, however, the well-known collector of that name. She married the Rev. John Rogers, through whose son it came into the possession of the niece of the latter. She married the Rev. Edward Edgell, rector of Rodden, Frome. The son of this gentleman, the Rev. E[dward] B[atenson] Edgell, late rector of Bromhead, sent the picture up to Christie's on June 24th, 1876, when it was bought in at £96 11 s[hillings]. After his death in 1904, it was placed with a firm of antique dealers in the country, who could obtain for it no higher offer than £30. It was brought to London, and sold at Christie's on May 12th, 1906, for £2,205, Sir Hugh Lane being the purchaser. The picture was generally accepted as a Titian, though it was also ascribed by various authorities to Giorgione, Sebastian del Piombo, Moretti [i.e., Moretto da Brescia], and other artists. Sir Hugh Lane sold the picture to Mr [Arthur] Grenfell for £30,000.[8]

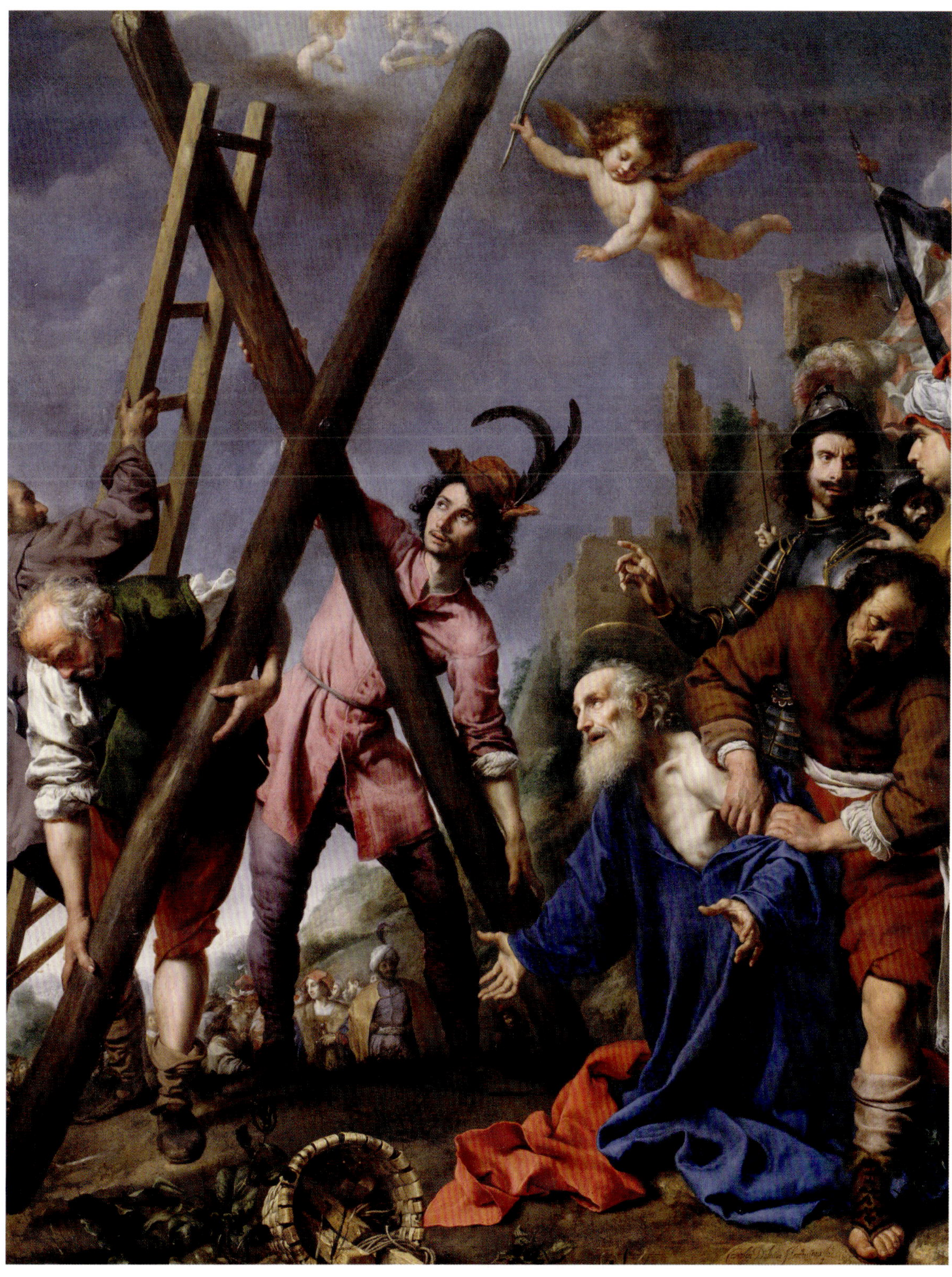

The reconstructions of 1906 and 1914 are mutually exclusive, and whether or not the provenance of 1906 was Brockwell's doing cannot be established. In any case, the source of the Methuen–Edgell provenance—recovered here for the first time—had been entirely forgotten by the late 1960s, when, despite many doubts, Frick curators included it in the new catalogue of the Italian paintings of the collection, published in 1968.[9] It has remained unquestioned ever since.

A rereading of Brockwell's articles today reveals that the hypothesis of a Methuen–Edgell provenance always lacked documentation. In Brockwell's letter to *The Times* of 1914, he himself wrote that while his genealogy of the Methuen family was based on written accounts, the information that "afford[ed] confirmation" of his findings was solely taken from "correspondence and interviews" with members of a collateral branch of the Methuen family. The little that is documented about the early history of the painting is that when it first appeared at auction on May 2, 1876, Titian's portrait was part of a sale of artworks from Foot's Cray Place.[10] Although duly reported in the 1906 *Times* article, this provenance subsequently disappeared from Brockwell's capricious reconstructions. Instead, the painting's documented provenance from Foot's Cray Place remains the only valid point of departure for a reconstruction of its early history.

From Florence to New York, via England

In 1924, the art historian Oskar Fischel noticed a figure painted after Titian's *Man in a Red Hat* in the background of the *St. Andrew Praying before His Martyrdom* by Carlo Dolci (1616–1686), several versions of which exist.[11] The Dolci picture had earlier been described by the seventeenth-century writer Filippo Baldinucci in his *Notizie de' professori del disegno* (1681–1728):

> Paolo del Sera, later a Florentine Senator, had a little story [*storietta*] of the martyrdom of St. Andrew the apostle, which he brought to Venice. And it was one of the earliest things ever to be seen in that city by his [i.e., Carlo Dolci's] hand. . . . Another similar story he carried out for Marchese Carlo Gerini, and one also for Carlo Corbinelli, which today belongs to the gentleman Andrea Rosso. . . . All three stories are of the same invention, though they are different in their dimensions.[12]

Paolo del Sera (1617–1672) was an art dealer who was instrumental in bringing countless Venetian paintings to Florence (and vice versa).[13] Among

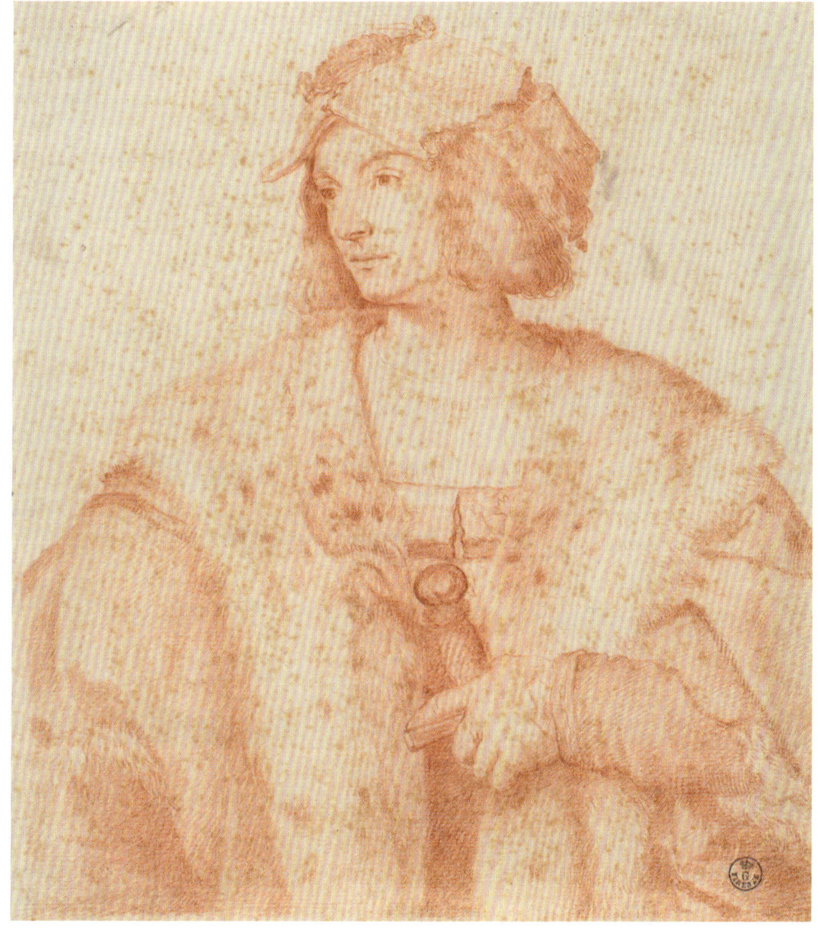

Fig. 3
Attributed to Carlo Dolci
Portrait of a Young Man
(after Titian's *Portrait of a Man in a Red Hat*), n.d.
Red chalk on paper
9 7/16 × 7 7/8 in. (240 × 200 mm)
Gabinetto dei Disegni e Stampe delle Gallerie degli Uffizi, Florence

his clients was Cardinal Leopoldo de' Medici, but Leopoldo may be ruled out as a former owner of the Frick portrait because it was never recorded in his collection or in that of his family.[14]

Three extant versions of Dolci's *Martyrdom* are commonly accepted as autograph.[15] It remains unclear if the version painted for Del Sera was a signed one of a rather large format (45½ × 36 in.) but on easily transportable canvas (fig. 2) or a smaller unsigned panel (20¾ × 16⅛ in.), now in a private collection in New York, which may better fit Baldinucci's description of a "storietta."[16] Whichever version of the *Martyrdom* belonged to Del Sera, all three include the figure after Titian's portrait at the Frick, as well as a turbaned man next to him that derives from a figure in the *Adoration of the Magi*, painted in Peter Paul Rubens's workshop.

Dolci had a penchant for quoting other painters' work but rarely left his hometown of Florence, his only documented travel being to Innsbruck in 1673.

As a result, his quotations were usually taken from Florentine works, although he also relied on suppliers to procure drawings from abroad.[17] A drawing of Titian's *Man in a Red Hat* in the Uffizi, which is generally accepted as by Dolci (fig. 3), offers a compelling clue to the provenance of the painting now at the Frick.[18] The fact that the colors of the figure in Dolci's painting match those of Titian's original—especially the red hat—suggests that Dolci may have had access to the canvas. Against this backdrop, the fanciful identification in the late nineteenth and early twentieth centuries of the sitter as Lorenzo de' Medici is yet another indication that the portrait may have had a Florentine provenance, as scholars have long suspected.

Strange as it may seem, this Florentine connection—incompatible with Brockwell's Methuen–Edgell provenance—dovetails perfectly with the indication that the painting came from Foot's Cray Place in 1876. A Palladian villa in Kent (fig. 4), Foot's Cray Place was unfortunately destroyed by a fire in 1949.[19] As stated in the *Times* article of 1906, the house was built in the mid-eighteenth century by (or for) Bourchier Cleeve (1715–1760) but, by 1821, had been sold to Nicholas Vansittart, 1st Baron Bexley (1776–1851).[20] Lord Bexley died childless, so his peerage became extinct, but he left Foot's Cray Place to his cousin Arthur Vansittart (1807–1859).[21]

Fig. 4
View of Foot's Cray Place (before 1949)

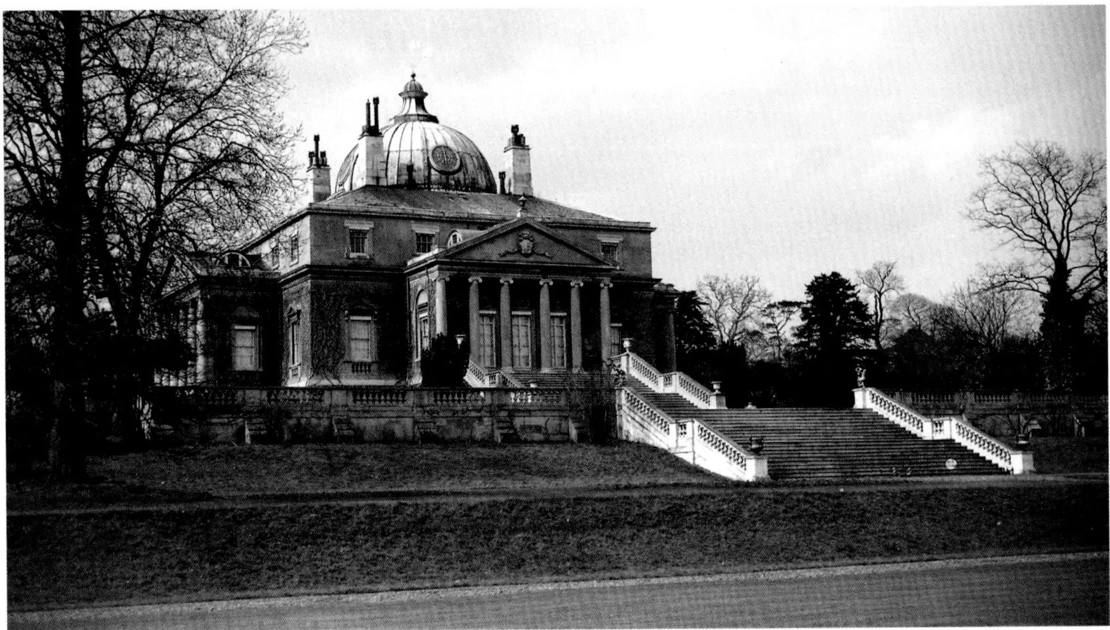

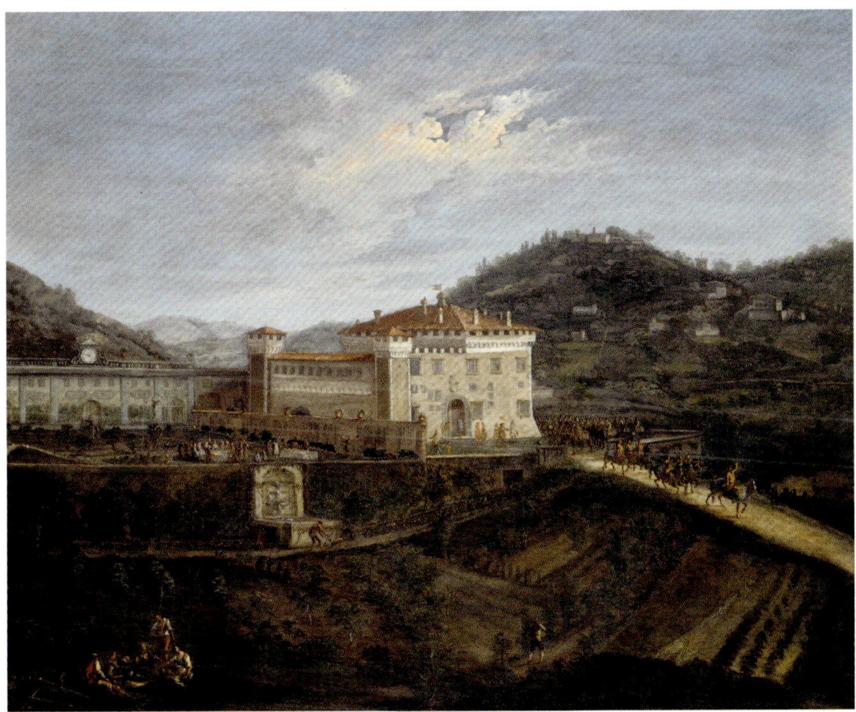

Fig. 5
Girolamo Costner
View of Villa Salviati alla Badia, 1710–16
Oil on canvas
28¾ × 34⅝ in. (73 × 88 cm)
Private collection

In 1844, Arthur Vansittart bought a large estate just outside Florence, Villa Salviati, which now houses the Historical Archives of the European Union. As the notarial act now confirms, the sale of the villa was made "at closed gates, that is, it includes all the furniture and the paintings etc."[22] In 1876, the same year the Titian was put up at auction, some artworks from Foot's Cray Place that are known to have shared an earlier provenance from Villa Salviati were also sold in London. They are a view of the villa itself (fig. 5) that can now be linked to payments to the painter Girolamo Costner between 1710 and 1716;[23] a portrait of Alamanno Salviati by Alessandro Allori;[24] and two portraits by Jacopo da Empoli, one of which is now at the Art Institute of Chicago.[25] In all likelihood, the portrait by Titian, long suspected to have come from Florence, shares the same provenance.

The Salviati paintings had made their way to England, probably before 1852, when Arthur Vansittart sold Villa Salviati to the Sardinian tenor Giovanni Matteo "Mario" De Candia.[26] By 1876, they had been inherited by Arthur's son, Captain Coleraine Robert Vansittart (1833–1886).[27] After fighting in the Crimean War (1853–56), Captain Vansittart—who was

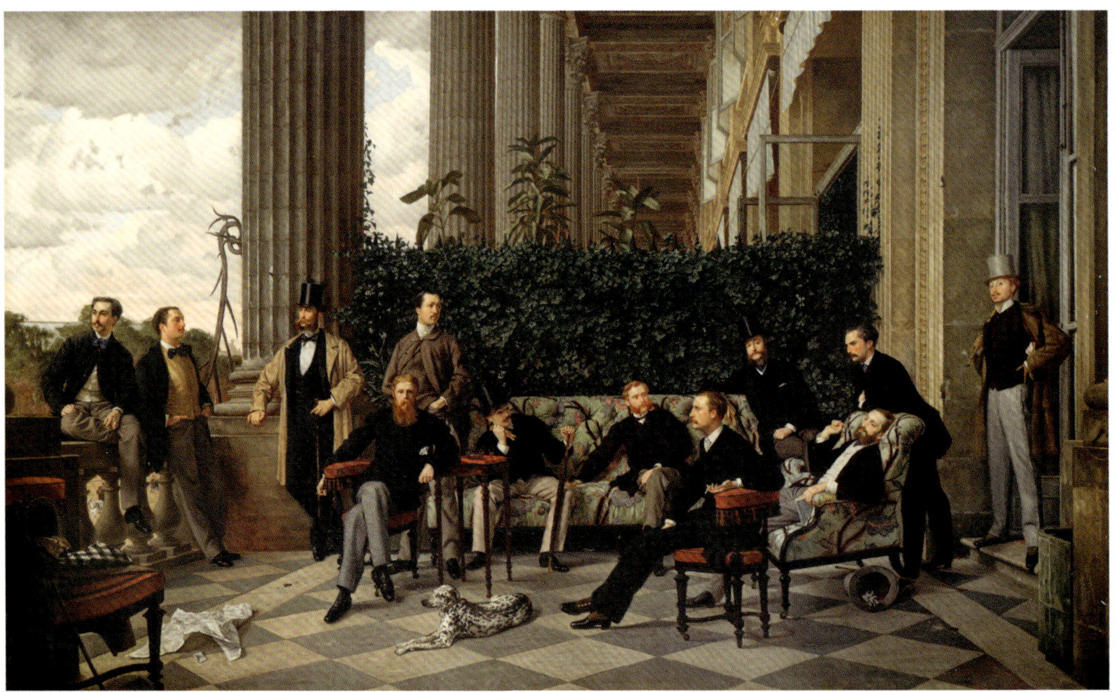

Fig. 6
Jacques Joseph Tissot
The Circle of the Rue Royale, 1868
Oil on canvas
68⅞ × 110⅝ in. (175 × 281 cm)
Musée d'Orsay, Paris

included in Jacques Joseph Tissot's famous group portrait *Circle of the Rue Royale* (fig. 6) as the red-haired gentleman in a chair—had settled in Paris.[28] In 1876, he decided to rent Foot's Cray Place to Sir John Pender, concurrently selling some of its artworks at auction.[29]

Unfortunately, the inventories of Villa Salviati prior to 1844 list the paintings—especially the portraits—in such a cursory manner that it is impossible to confirm the precise moment when the Frick portrait may have entered the Salviati collection (or indeed whether it ever did).[30] Nonetheless, it is tempting to speculate that the Salviatis purchased the painting in the 1630s directly from Paolo del Sera, who was closely associated with the Salviati family. Not only did Paolo and the Salviatis live on the same street in Florence—Via Ghibellina—but Del Sera wrote in an unpublished letter of 1646 that Marchese Vincenzo Salviati had "always protected and favored [him] in all things, as if [he] w[ere] his son."[31]

It therefore seems likely that the painting now at the Frick was in Florence, in the Salviati collection, already in the seventeenth century. If so, it was brought there by Paolo del Sera, who may have wanted a small copy of Titian's portrait—a souvenir of sorts—to be included in the painting he commissioned from Dolci. Brought to England before 1852 by Arthur Vansittart, the Titian picture was sold at auction in London by his son in 1876 together with a group of other Florentine artworks. It is interesting to note here that if Titian's *Portrait of a Man in a Red Hat* did indeed come from Villa Salviati, one of its former owners would have been Camillo Borghese (1775–1832), Napoleon's brother-in-law, whose portrait by François Gérard is at the Frick. In 1809, following the death of his mother, Anna Maria Salviati, Camillo inherited the villa, which he in turn left to his brother Francesco (1776–1839) at his own death, childless, in 1832. It was precisely Francesco's children—Marcantonio Borghese (1814–1886), Camillo Aldobrandini (1816–1902), and Scipione Salviati (1823–1892)—who sold the villa to Vansittart in 1844.[32]

Coleraine R. Vansittart's sale of May 1876, which included the portrait of "Lorenzo the Magnificent" by Titian, had been set up by a judge in order to settle a legal dispute between the captain and some of his relatives.[33] Held by Christie's on the premises of Foot's Cray Place, the sale came to be known as the "Bexley sale," while in fact many of the lots had been acquired by Coleraine and Arthur Vansittart, not their distant relative, the late Lord Bexley. The Titian painting was sold on May 2 for £71 and 8 shillings to a "Waters"—in all likelihood the "S. Waters" who was an agent in London at the time.[34] Less than two months later, on June 24, the portrait reappeared as part of a miscellaneous sale at Christie's, London, where it fetched about £90—an increase certainly worth Waters's time.[35] The buyer, an "Owens" according to an annotated copy of the catalogue from the National Art Library in London, eludes precise identification. If Brockwell is to be trusted—at least as far as the most recent chapter in the history of Titian's painting is concerned—it is possible that the canvas was later acquired by Edward Batenson Edgell (1820–1904). In which case, after the latter's death, his son Edward Methuen Rogers Edgell (1851–1916) may have inherited it.[36] Whatever the vagaries of its provenance since 1876, only in 1906 did Titian's *Man in a Red Hat* resurface at auction, again at Christie's in London: its seller unknown, it was still identified as the portrait of Lorenzo de' Medici, which all commentators connected to the "Bexley" sale of 1876.[37] It was then bought for £2,205 by Sir Hugh Lane (1875–1915), the Irish aesthete, art collector, and dealer.[38]

Lane used to complain that he was not a good fit for the job of selling paintings, once writing: "I don't understand selling. That's my great trouble. I've got to buy pictures without money and to sell them without conviction."[39] Yet, over the years following his purchase of the Titian, he managed to successfully coordinate a press campaign to add prestige (and value) to the newly restored

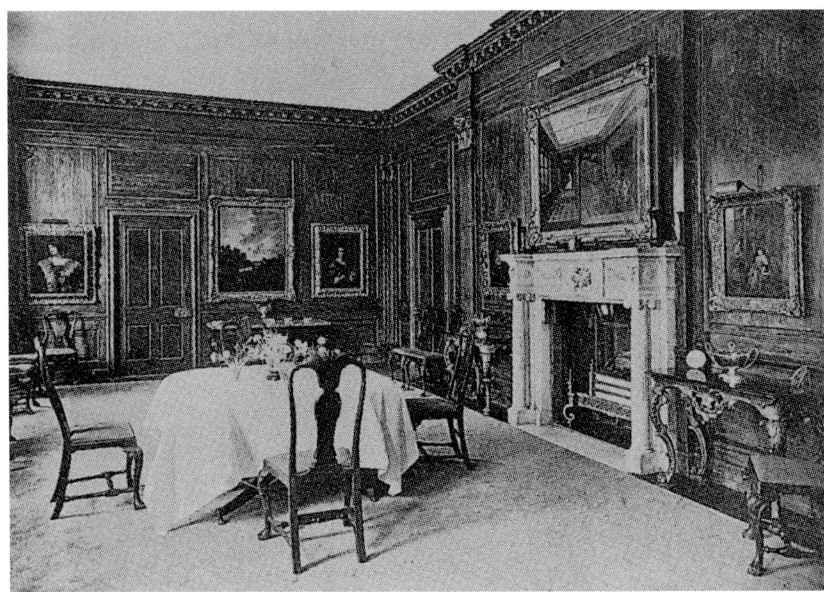

Fig. 7
View of Roehampton House, London, before 1914 (with Titian's *Portrait of a Man in a Red Hat* hanging on the wall)
From Weedon et al. 1996

painting—part of which, one suspects, may have been Brockwell's research into the provenance.[40] Lane's initiatives resulted in a sensational increase in the value of the painting, as recorded in *The Times* in 1911:

> We are informed that Sir Hugh Lane has sold his well-known Titian portrait, "A Man in a Red Cap," to an English collector for £30,000. The picture will remain in England. . . . For a picture which, a century or so ago, cost only a few hundred guineas, to change hands in these days at five and six figures is not a very extraordinary circumstance. But to purchase a picture at 2,100 guineas and to sell it in less than five years at £30,000, and that not to the ever-present American millionaire, is an achievement quite out the usual run.[41]

Lane's strategy was in fact aimed at selling his paintings to affluent American collectors such as Henry Clay Frick (1849–1919).[42] And the "English collector" in whose London home the portrait by Titian had landed—Roehampton House (fig. 7)—was Arthur Morton Grenfell (1873–1958), a banker who owed his wealth to American investments.[43]

Grenfell's mining and railway investments in Canada turned out to be badly timed, and he was forced to declare bankruptcy in 1914. This led to the auctioning of his personal property to cover his debts. Obeying what he believed to be a dealer's code of honor, Lane bought back the paintings he had sold to Grenfell at the latter's June 1914 estate sale, where he secured Titian's portrait—now identified as a portrait of Lorenzo de' Medici, Duke of Urbino (1492–1519)—for about £13,000.[44] However, since Lane was then completely broke and could not afford to purchase the Titian, it was kept in the storeroom at Christie's awaiting payment.[45] At this point, Lane hired the Englishwoman Henriette Lewis Hind as a selling agent. Hind was friends with Alice Creelman in New York, an acquaintance of Henry Clay Frick's.[46] On April 2, 1915, Creelman wrote to Frick that Hind had access to "a small collection of wonderful paintings belonging to a titled man who had been ruined by the war"—that is, Hugh Lane. Among the paintings on sale were a "beautiful Titian, *really* beautiful" and a "superb Holbein." The latter was the *Thomas Cromwell* (now at the Frick), on which Frick had set his eyes the previous year but had turned down at £60,000. The price now was $290,000 for the Holbein and $150,000 for the Titian, soon reduced to $365,000 for both. On April 25, 1915, following some brutal negotiations, during which Frick showed that his interest lay mainly in the Holbein, Creelman wrote that both paintings had been shipped: the Titian on the motorship *St. Louis* (fig. 8) and the Holbein on the *Philadelphia*.[47] Upon receipt of the paintings,

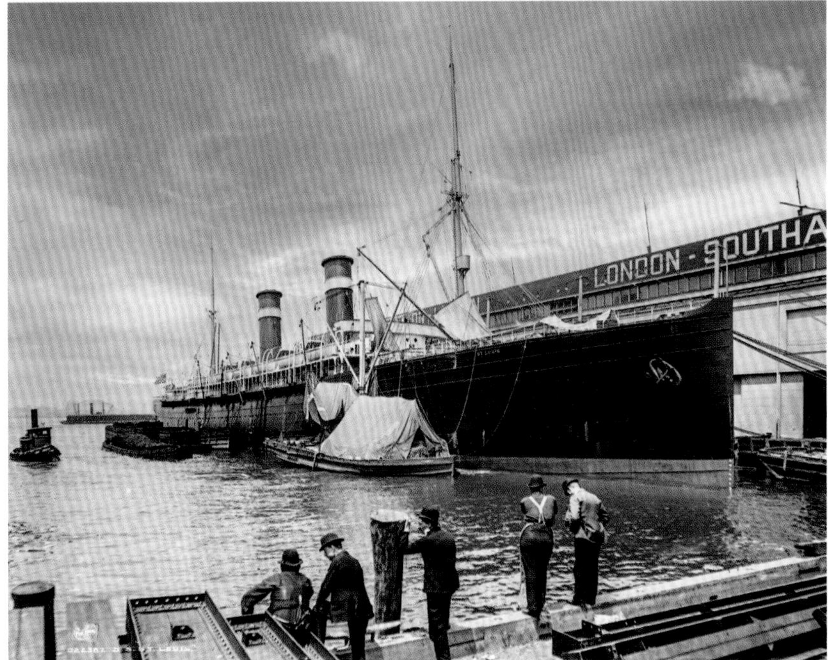

Fig. 8
The SS *St. Louis* of the American Line (launched 1895) at Southampton Landing Stage

Fig. 9
Giorgione (Giorgio da Castelfranco)
Portrait of a Man, 1506
Oil on panel
11⅞ × 10⅛ in. (30.2 × 25.7 cm)
The San Diego Museum of Art; Gift of Anne R. and Amy Putnam

on May 18, Frick issued an order of payment for £60,000 (corresponding to $287,850) for both the Holbein and the Titian ($215,000 and $72,850, respectively), to which he added a $26,663.67 fee for Creelman.

On April 21, 1915, Sir Hugh Lane, who was staying at the St. Regis in New York, wrote to Frick to ask if he would consider sitting for a portrait by John Singer Sargent (which he sadly did not). In the letter, he also congratulated him on the "bargain" of the Holbein and Titian, although he confessed that he was "angry with Mrs Hind for giving [him] to understand that the portraits were being sold to someone I did not know, as there is no reason why we should not have done the deal direct!" On May 7, 1915, two days before the *St. Louis* carrying the Titian docked in New York, Lane died at sea when his homebound ship, the *Lusitania*, was torpedoed and sunk by German U-boats—an event that highlights the perils of seafaring travels during World War I and also helps to explain why the paintings were insured and shipped on separate boats.[48] When the *Man in a Red Hat* arrived at the Frick, it was installed in the Living Hall, where it came to complement the wall with Bellini's *St. Francis in the Desert* and Titian's *Pietro Aretino*, and where it remained for the ensuing century.

Young Titian and Giorgione

Soon after the portrait reached the Frick mansion at 1 East 70th Street, its attribution began to swing between Titian and Giorgione.[49] Apparently, Carel F. L. de Wild made a persuasive case for the attribution to Giorgione in a now-lost report to Frick of 1918.[50] In Frick's postmortem estate inventory of 1920, the painting was listed as "also attributed to Giorgione" and valued at $60,000.[51] The *Man in a Red Hat* had to wait until the 1950s for its attribution to settle again on Titian.[52] However, the portrait is often labeled in the literature as one of the most "Giorgionesque" among Titian's works.[53] Because this characterization has impacted both the interpretation and chronology of the painting, the term "Giorgionesque" requires some qualification in the context of this book. Who was Giorgione and how did his work influence Titian?

Very little is known about Giorgione (1473/74–1510).[54] Few documents survive about his life, and, as far as his works are concerned, only four can be assigned to him with certainty: a portrait of an unidentified sitter now in San Diego, formerly in the Terris collection (fig. 9); the famous *Tempest* at the

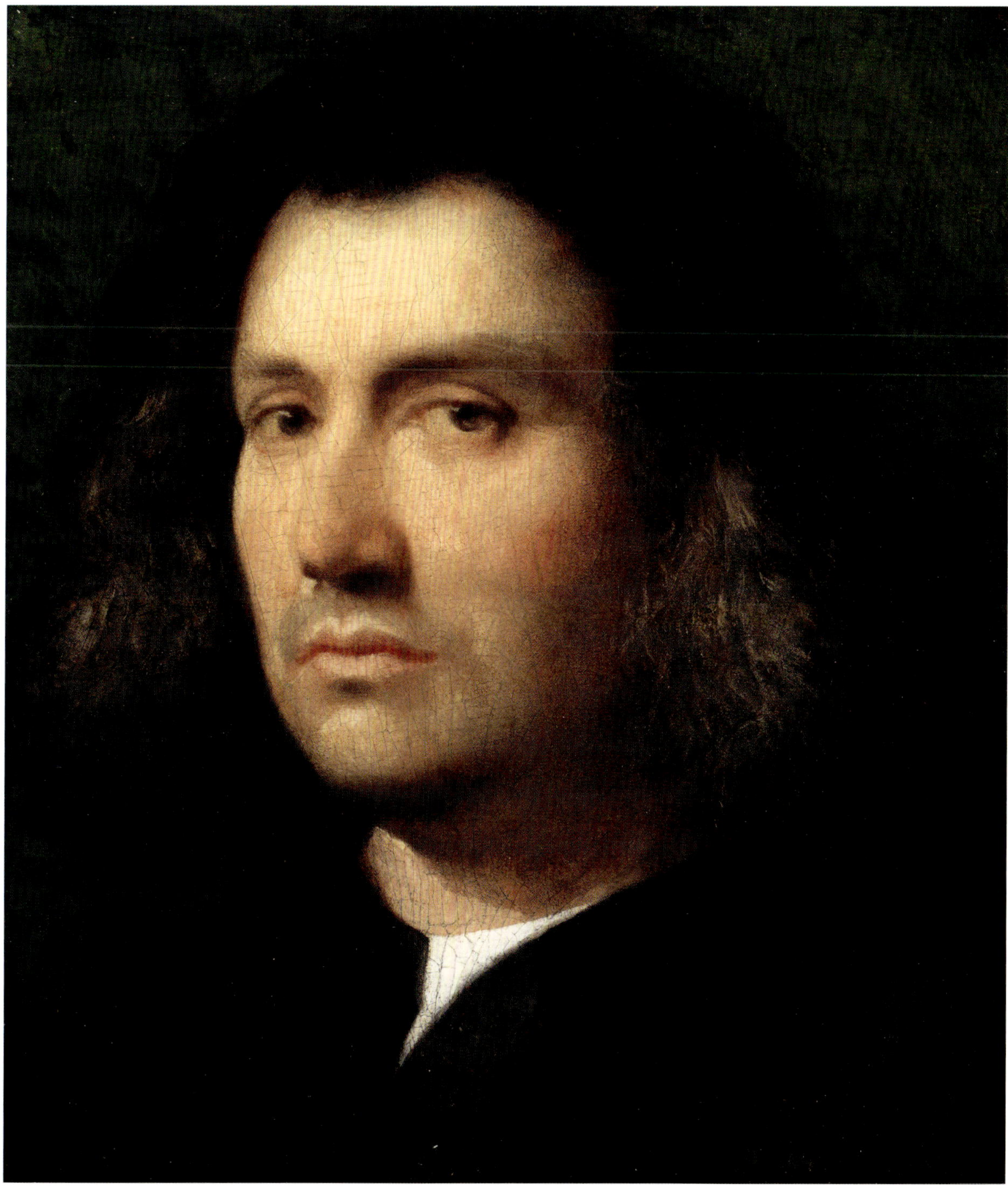

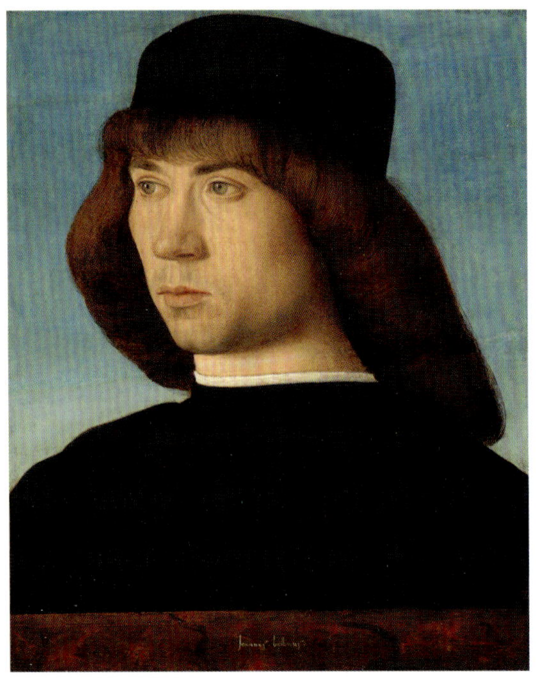

Gallerie dell'Accademia in Venice; the so-called *Laura* of 1506 at the Kunsthistorisches Museum in Vienna; and, in the same museum, the *Three Philosophers*.[55] Works such as these would have been unthinkable fifteen or twenty years before they were painted. A simple comparison between the Terris portrait and a typical, if very high quality, portrait by Bellini from the 1490s (fig. 10) illustrates the enormous changes that Venetian painting—and portraits in particular—underwent at the turn of the century, creating new "formal solutions not significantly added to until the age of Degas."[56] The brushstrokes have softened, the sharp contours have blurred, and the sitter stands in a different relation to the viewer. Most important, the portrait has been emancipated from its formal dependence on the sculpted bust or the medal, and the eyes have come to play a crucial role in the drama of the painting, with the turning pose of the sitter introducing a dimension of temporality to the picture. The evenly lit window view onto an open landscape is replaced by a dramatically lit interior. Overall, the emotional tone of the picture has changed. These new portraits align closely with Leonardo's prescriptions as to how to paint a successful portrait:

Fig. 10
Giovanni Bellini
Portrait of a Young Man, ca. 1490
Oil on panel (poplar)
12 3/16 × 9 3/4 in. (30.9 × 24.8 cm)
National Gallery of Art, Washington; Samuel H. Kress Collection

Fig. 11
Albrecht Dürer
Portrait of a Young Man, 1506
Oil on panel
18 1/8 × 13 3/4 in. (46 × 35 cm)
Musei di Strada Nuova–Palazzo Rosso, Genoa

> When you wish to portray someone, do so in dull weather, towards the evening, having the sitter keep their back to one of the walls of a courtyard. Pay attention to the faces of men and women in the street, as the night draws in, when the weather is bad—how much grace and sweetness [*grazia e dolcezza*] is in their faces.[57]

Indeed, Leonardo (1452–1519) and, through him, Giorgione, have traditionally been credited with having had a transformative impact on Venetian painting of these years. As Giorgio Vasari put it in his *Lives*:

> [Giorgione] studied drawing [*disegno*] and relished it. And in this [i.e., *disegno*] nature favored him so highly, that he, having become enamored of her beauties and imitating her so much, acquired the name not only of having surpassed Giovanni and Gentile Bellini, but also of being the rival

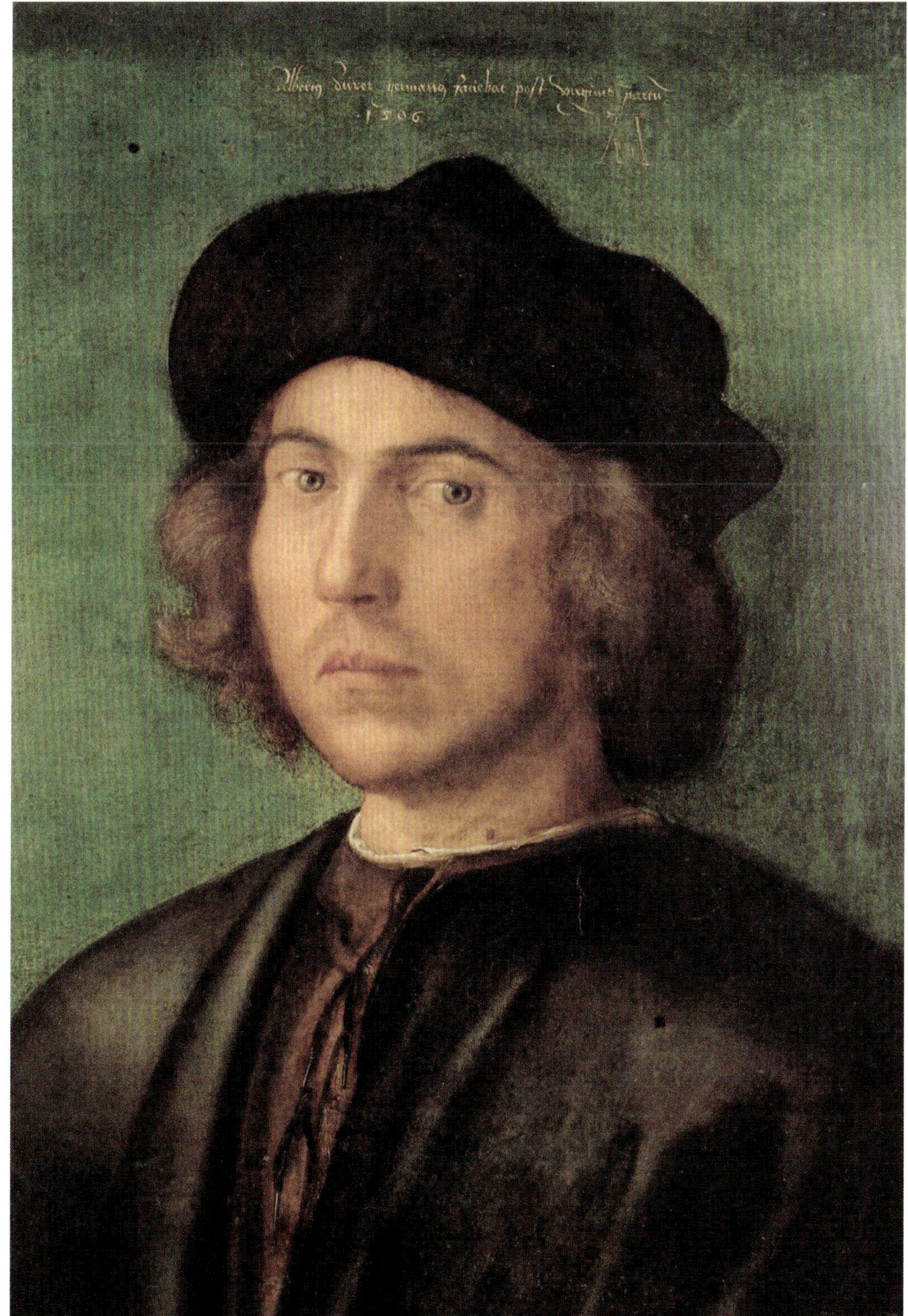

Fig. 12
Hans Memling
Portrait of a Man from the Lespinette Family, 1480s
Oil on panel
11⅞ × 8¾ in. (30.1 × 22.3 cm)
Mauritshuis, The Hague

> of the masters who were working in Tuscany and were the creators of the modern manner [*maniera moderna*]. Giorgione had seen some things by the hand of Leonardo, very nuanced and terribly dark: and this manner pleased him so much that he was forever studying it as long as he lived, and imitated it greatly in the colors of oil painting.[58]

Giorgione is also believed to have imparted to Titian the tools with which to become a great painter:

> Titian, then, having seen the method and manner of Giorgione, abandoned the manner of Giambellino [i.e., Giovanni Bellini] although he had consumed much time with it, and attached himself to that [of Giorgione]; coming in a short time to imitate his [i.e., Giorgione's] works so well, that his pictures at times were mistaken for Giorgione's. . . . At the time when he first began to follow Giorgione's manner, not being more than eighteen, he made the portrait of a gentleman friend of his from the Barbarigo household.[59]

This Leonardo–Giorgione–Titian genealogy, which seems confirmed by historical data, has long intrigued art historians. On the one hand, Leonardo was in Venice in the year 1500—having fled Milan, which had been invaded by the French—and likely had contacts with Venetian artists. On the other hand, Titian and Giorgione worked at roughly the same time on the frescoes of the facade of the Fondaco dei Tedeschi, in Venice (mostly lost).

Scholars, however, have rightfully insisted that the Fondaco commission, for which Titian and Giorgione devised distinct iconographic programs, was awarded independently to the two artists.[60] Furthermore, Leonardo was just one among many foreign artists to bring about significant changes during sojourns in the city on the lagoon. Between 1490 and 1510, scores of artists of varied backgrounds (and standing) resided in Venice, including Perugino (1494–97), Albrecht Dürer (1494–95; 1506–7), Cristoforo and Andrea Solario (1492–95), Giovanni Agostino da Lodi (ca. 1495–1506), Mantegna (1506), Boccaccio Boccaccino (1506), and Fra Bartolomeo (1508). Moreover, works by Hieronymus Bosch and Hans Memling made their way into the collections of Venetian patricians during the same period.[61] Against this background, a comparison between Giorgione's Terris portrait (see fig. 9), usually dated 1506, and a portrait by Dürer in Genoa of that same year (fig. 11) or an earlier portrait by Memling (fig. 12) suffices to illustrate the complexity of reciprocal influences.[62]

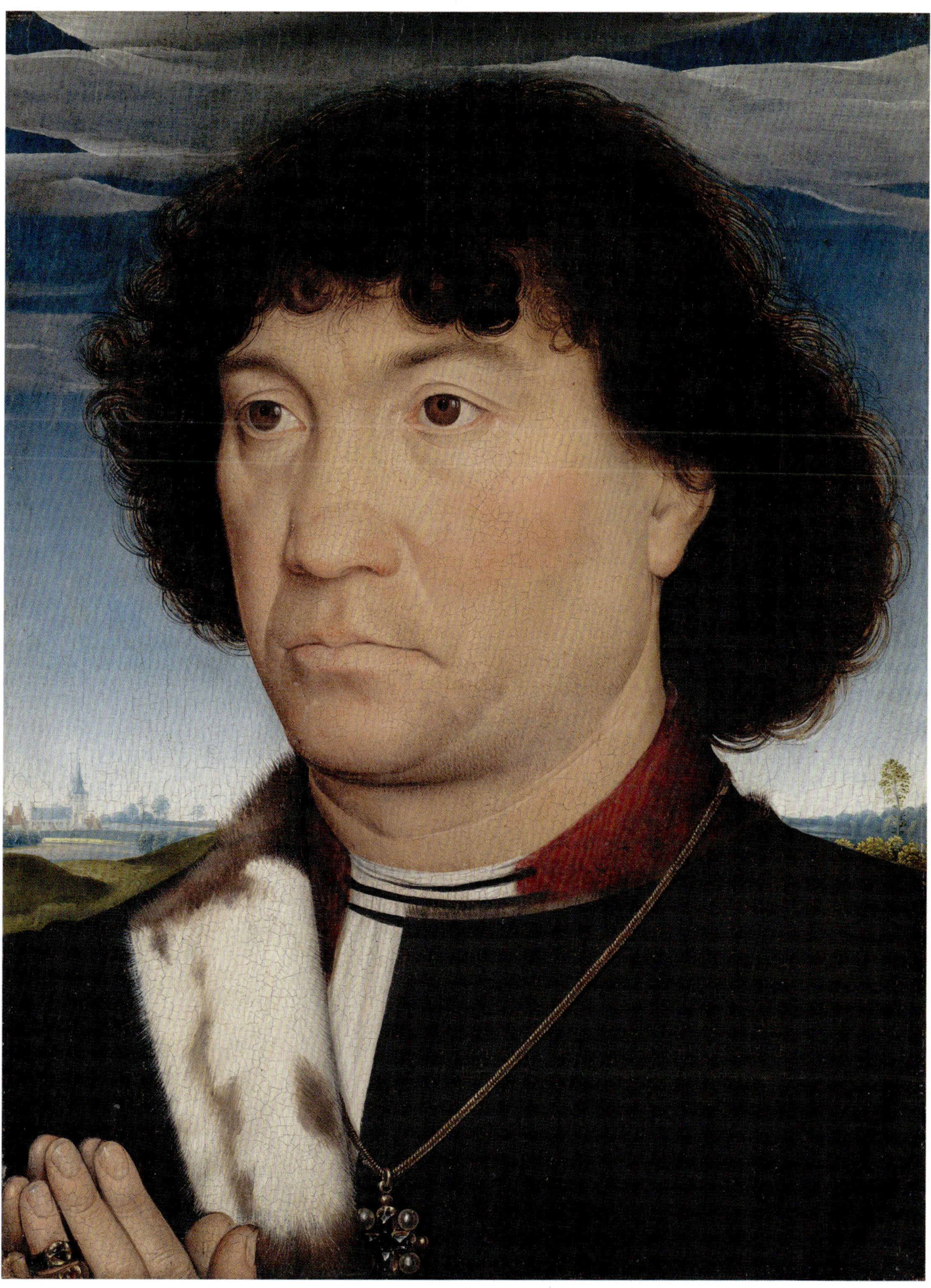

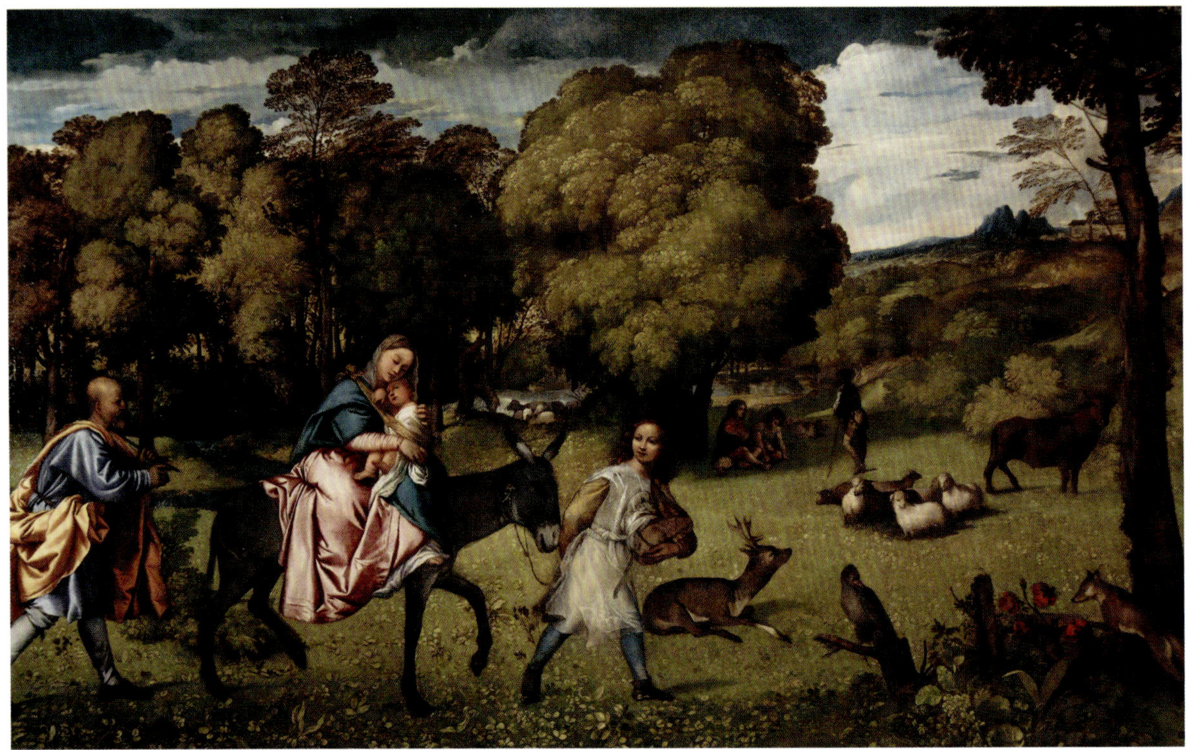

Fig. 13
Titian (Tiziano Vecellio)
The Flight into Egypt, 1506/7
Oil on canvas
80 5⁄16 × 127 3⁄4 in.
(204 × 324.5 cm) excluding
17th-century additions
Hermitage Museum,
St. Petersburg

Young Titian's Venice was a much more cosmopolitan environment than Vasari would have us think. Very little, if anything, is known about Titian's youth other than his birth in Pieve di Cadore, in the mountains northwest of Venice, possibly between 1488 and 1490. When he came to Venice as a young apprentice, he is likely to have benefited from the stimulating pictorial environment he encountered there. Titian's education would have extended well beyond Giorgione's tutelage, and he must also have conducted a peer-to-peer dialogue with his colleagues, among them Sebastiano del Piombo (1485–1547), another pupil of Giorgione's, before the latter's departure for Rome in 1510. A comparison of two large canvases of similar dimension, in all likelihood painted for the *portego* (passage hall) of Ca' Loredan in 1506/7—the *Flight into Egypt* by Titian in the Hermitage (fig. 13) and the *Judgement of Solomon* by Sebastiano at Kingston Lacy (fig. 14)[63]—illustrates at least two important points: the variety of stylistic possibilities available to young Venetian artists at the time and the potential for mutual learning among young artists of the same generation.

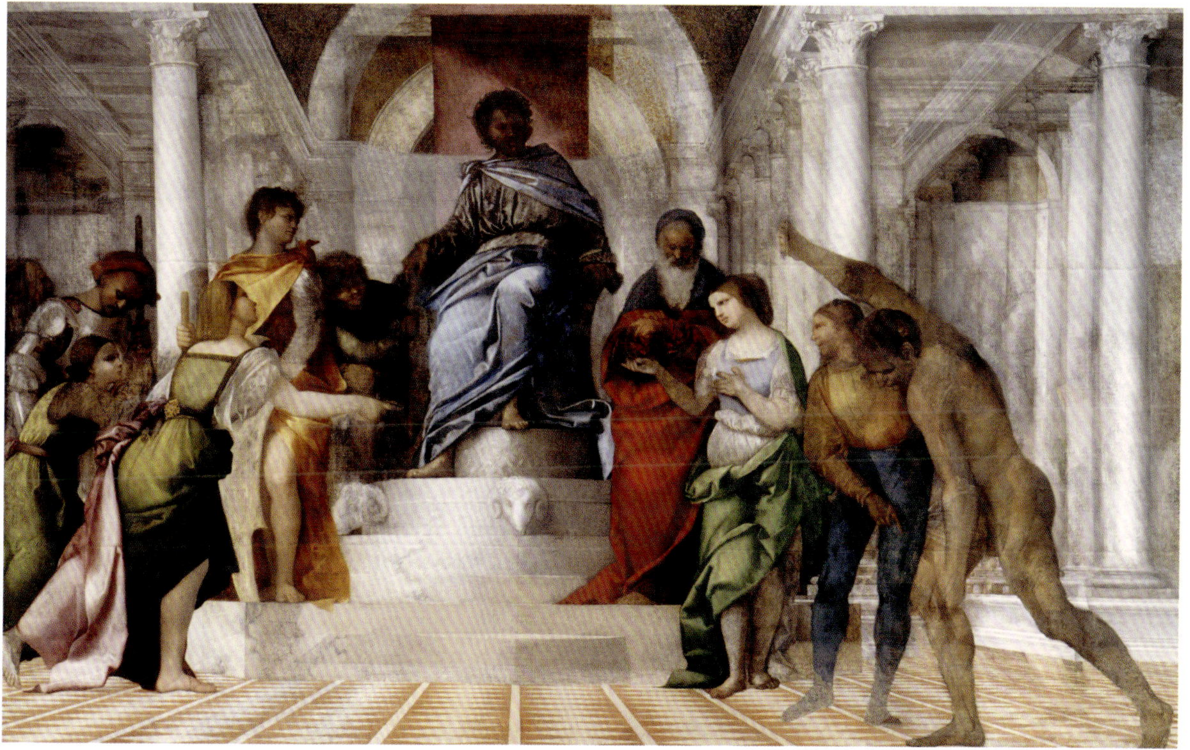

Fig. 14
Sebastiano del Piombo
(Sebastiano Luciani)
The Judgement of Solomon, 1506/7
Oil on canvas
81⅞ × 124 in. (208 × 315 cm)
The National Trust Collections, Kingston Lacy, Wimborne

An interpretation very distant from Vasari's of Giorgione's importance for Titian emerges from Lodovico Dolce's *Dialogo della pittura* of 1557. While agreeing that Titian had in fact trained with Giorgione, Dolce massively rescaled the impact of such training:

> Granted, it is a miracle that, without as yet having then seen the antiquities of Rome, which were a source of enlightenment to all excellent painters, and purely by dint of that little tiny spark which he had discovered in Giorgione's works, Titian saw, and became acquainted with, the essence of perfect painting.[64]

Dolce's text is often framed as a reaction to the first edition of Vasari's *Lives* (1550). In fact, scholars have demonstrated that Dolce's treatise was written long before Vasari's went to press.[65] As to Vasari's account of Giorgione's practice in his *Lives*, the many inconsistencies between the first (1550) and second (1568) edition—and also within the second edition—warrant some caution in accepting his framing of Giorgione as a follower of Leonardo, which may

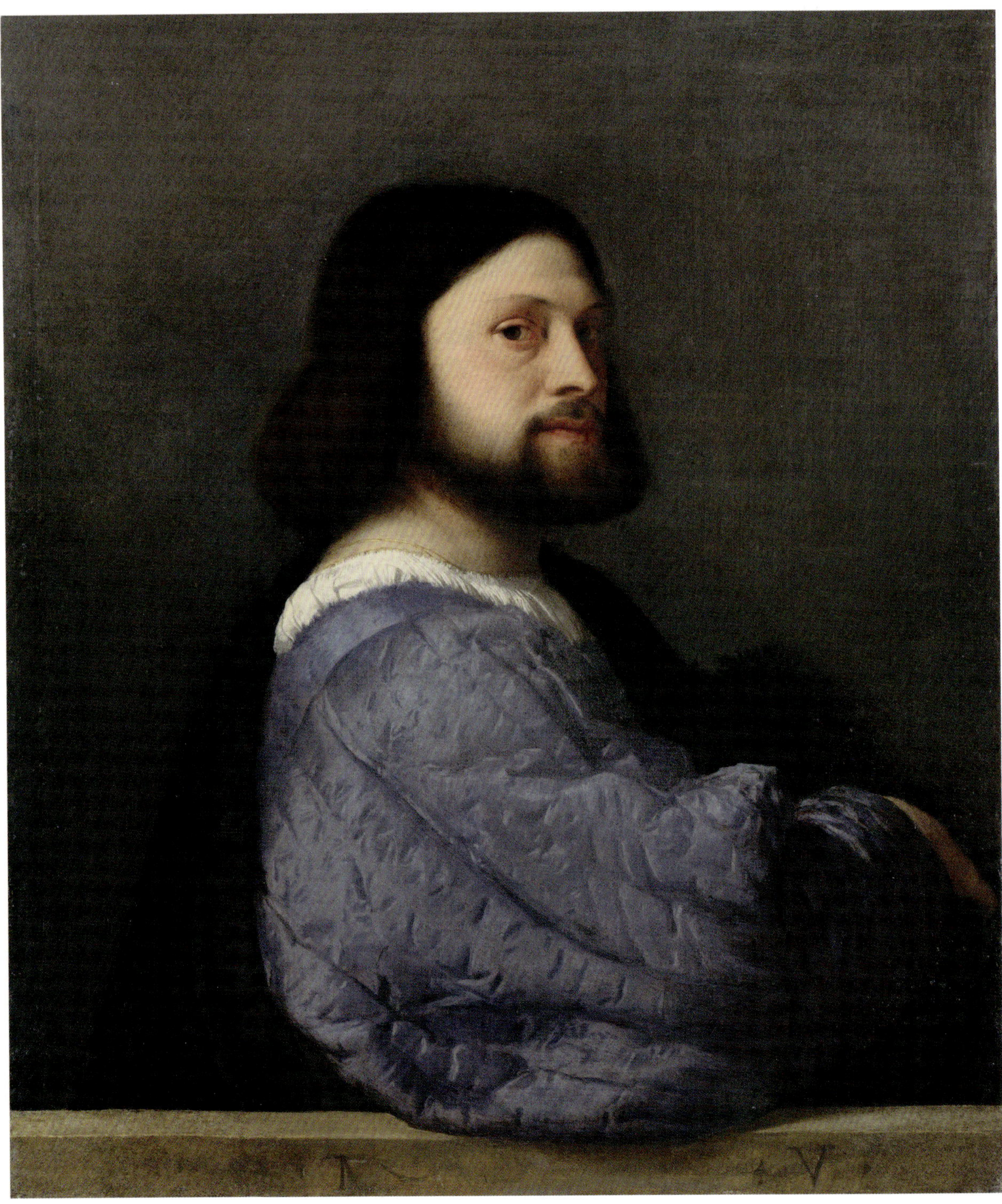

be due more to historiographical concerns than to historical reality.[66] All in all, Vasari conveys a confused idea of Giorgione: while modern critics praise him for his ability to achieve the presence of forms by means of smooth transitions in areas of delineation, Vasari, in both the first and second editions of the *Lives*, perplexingly praised Giorgione for his *disegno*, only to later glaringly contradict himself by saying, in his account of Titian's life, that Giorgione had painted "without *disegno*," in keeping with other Venetian artists whom he understood to prioritize color over drawing.[67] As Francis Haskell pointed out, Vasari's Giorgione may have been far less "lyrical" than the Giorgione of modern scholars.[68]

Fig. 15
Titian (Tiziano Vecellio)
Gerolamo (?) *Barbarigo*, ca. 1510
Oil on canvas
31¹⁵⁄₁₆ × 26⅛ in.
(81.2 × 66.3 cm)
The National Gallery, London

Tom Nichols recently suggested that while Giorgione is often framed "as a convenient linking figure in a wider and coherent historical narrative," Titian's and Sebastiano's "sympathy for his approach was relatively brief."[69] Whether a linchpin of Titian's training or a more minor figure in his development, Giorgione ceased to exert whatever active role he had in Titian's education when he died in 1510. His glorification was mostly a posthumous affair, with all the attendant historiographical difficulties.[70] After many centuries, it is difficult to measure the impact of Giorgione's art on Titian. Comparison of a portrait by Titian at the earliest stage of his career, which has been persuasively identified as the "gentleman friend of his from the Barbarigo household" mentioned by Vasari (fig. 15),[71] and the Terris portrait by Giorgione (see fig. 9) illustrates Titian's debt to Giorgione as much as it demonstrates Titian's independence from the older master in terms of format, monumentality, color, syntax, sharpness of drawing, and intensity in the dialogue with the beholder.

"Giorgionesque," that inadequate shorthand often used to characterize Titian's youthful works, clearly overplays Giorgione's influence on young Titian, but it does point to two salient characteristics of the latter's early work: first, the softness of brushstrokes and the artist's interest in the blurry contours between light and shadow (close to Leonardo's *sfumato*); second, a high degree of psychological insightfulness in portraits, a theme that warrants further discussion.

The "Hamlet of the Lagoons"

In spring 1498, Isabella d'Este (1474–1539), Marchioness of Mantua, wrote to her friend Cecilia Gallerani to ask her to send the latter's portrait by Leonardo (the famous *Lady with the Ermine*) to Mantua so she could compare it with some unspecified portraits by Giovanni Bellini.[72] The outcome of this comparison has not been recorded, but Isabella soon started to pester Leonardo to make her portrait. The following year, Leonardo was in Mantua, where he painted her. In March 1500, Lorenzo da Pavia, a Venetian correspondent of Isabella's, informed the marchioness that "Leonardo Vinci, who showed me a portrait of Your Lordship which is very similar [*naturale*] to You, is here in Venice."[73]

This episode is significant for several reasons. First, it attests to the circulation of Leonardo's works in Mantua and Venice. Second, the Bellini–Leonardo comparison illuminates the way the most sophisticated art patrons of the time were reframing the dialogue between artists as a competition. Third, it shows that portraits were seen as a privileged means to judge this competition and were becoming increasingly prized possessions. Scholars have tied such demand to the new expectation that portraits not merely record a sitter's looks but also capture their *moti dell'animo* (vagaries of the spirit). As Leonardo himself put it:

> Human figures should [be represented as] acting in keeping with what they are doing, so that, upon seeing them, you can understand what they are thinking or saying; all of which will be learnt well by those who imitate the gestures of those who are mute, who speak with the movements of the hands, of the eyes and eyebrows and of their whole body, when they want to express the idea of their spirit [*concetto de l'animo loro*].[74]

Though probably not quite as abrupt as art-historical narratives describe it, this shift in portrait painting, as well as in the collecting of portraits, was fostered by cultural and historical circumstances peculiar to the dawn of the Cinquecento in Venice.[75]

Lina Bolzoni, among others, has demonstrated that it was in dialogue (and competition) with poetry that portraits became an arena in which to negotiate the visibility of feelings.[76] Specifically, this new conception of portraiture developed a longstanding poetic trope of the window looking onto the soul, trespassing the barrier of the body as a "veil to the soul" (Petrarch). This change occurred at a time when a "new civilization" was founded on vernacular literacy, printing, and the book; a civilization that—the elderly of Venice often protested—tended to withdraw from the humdrum duties of public life and became more inclined than previous generations to luxury clothing, sexual misconduct (or what was perceived as such), and literary pursuits.[77] John Shearman describes how the Frick portrait uniquely embodies these cultural and sociological changes:

> This young man represents for me the *jeunesse dorée* of the Venetian republic, who made the older generation apoplectic during the dangerous wars of the League of Cambrai [1508–16], and this Hamlet of the Lagoons seems rather self-indulgently to have chosen to be sicklied o'er with the pale cast of thought. But his sentiment may remind us that his was the generation that invented the madrigal, the genre where self-pity is the dominant affectation.[78]

Building on a passage in Vasari where Giorgione is said to have "continually delighted in the things of love," scholars have long debated the link between Giorgione's portraiture and *Gli Asolani*, a book written in the vernacular by Pietro Bembo between 1497 and 1504, which was published for the first time the following year by Aldo Manuzio in Venice.[79] Set at the court of Caterina Cornaro, the former queen of Cyprus in Asolo (on the Venetian mainland), *Gli Asolani* consists of three dialogues on the nature of love. Some have it that *Gli Asolani* is nothing short of a manifesto of "Giorgionesque" portraiture.[80] Others believe that *Gli Asolani* contributed to putting an end to melancholic portraiture like Giorgione's or young Titian's, advocating for detachment and decorum in one's love life, which ultimately found expression some years later in Baldassare Castiglione's *Il Cortegiano* (1513–24, published 1528), a philosophical dialogue on the topic of what constitutes an ideal courtier.[81] Here, Castiglione protested the emotional affectation of many courtiers:

> I would have our Courtier's face . . . not so soft and feminine as many attempt to have who not only curl their hair and pluck their eyebrows, but preen themselves in all those ways that the most lecherous and shameless women in the world adopt; and in walking, in posture, and in every act, appear so flaccid and languid that their limbs seem to be on the verge of falling apart; and utter their words so limply that it seems that they are about to expire on the spot.[82]

Perhaps the truth is somewhere in the middle. Undeniably, there are passages in *Gli Asolani* that seem to capture portraits such as the *Man in a Red Hat*:

> No beautiful young man do I ever see in the street, walking alone one step after another, pensive, and self-contained, without considering: "Perhaps, he is thinking of his woman."[83]

But because the book had a long gestation and, by virtue of its structure, spanned new and old conceptions of love, it remains unclear what kind of portraiture Bembo and his friends favored.[84] And, it is more than likely that different strands in portraiture coexisted at the same time and for the same patrons.

Whether Bembo's *Asolani* is reflected in, or contributed to extinguishing, melancholic Venetian portraiture of the early sixteenth century—or both—the book is undeniably the manifesto of a moment when the discussion around love was perceived as a fundamental marker of the persona of any member of the cultivated elite. Titian seems to have been in touch with such patrons more than Giorgione ever was and was more likely to produce portraits appealing to them.[85] By the time *Il Cortegiano* became a textbook of the sophisticated lifestyle, however, Titian's portraits, if technically consistent with his earlier production, had become "virtuoso depictions of identity as social representation," firmly establishing the character of his sitters as successful men of consequence.[86] Like *Gli Asolani*, Titian's *Man in a Red Hat*, often seen as an early, purely "Giorgionesque" work, may in fact sit somewhere between these two categories of portraits: it sustains the sitter's sense of rank, while subordinating it to his personal presence. In negotiating between psychological insightfulness (and the softness of the painting that went with it) and the sitter's social standing, it communicates to the viewer that the juvenile persona of its sitter was itself in the process of being fashioned by a new culture of appearances.[87]

A New Chronology

Most scholars have argued that Titian's *Man in a Red Hat* dates from either the first half of the 1510s or about 1516.[88] This is because the *Man in a Red Hat* is usually dated in relation to two other pictures: *The Pastoral Concert* (fig. 16), dated 1510 or thereabout, and *Portrait of a Youth* (fig. 17), usually dated 1516.[89] Both parallels are, however, inconclusive.

The patronage and original destination of *The Pastoral Concert* remain unknown, and its authorship is traditionally given either to Giorgione or to a very young Titian.[90] It is usually dated 1510, the year of Giorgione's death, simply because this is either the closest Giorgione ever looks like Titian or, conversely, the closest Titian ever looks like Giorgione. In the painting is a figure wearing a red hat who is often compared with the sitter of the Frick

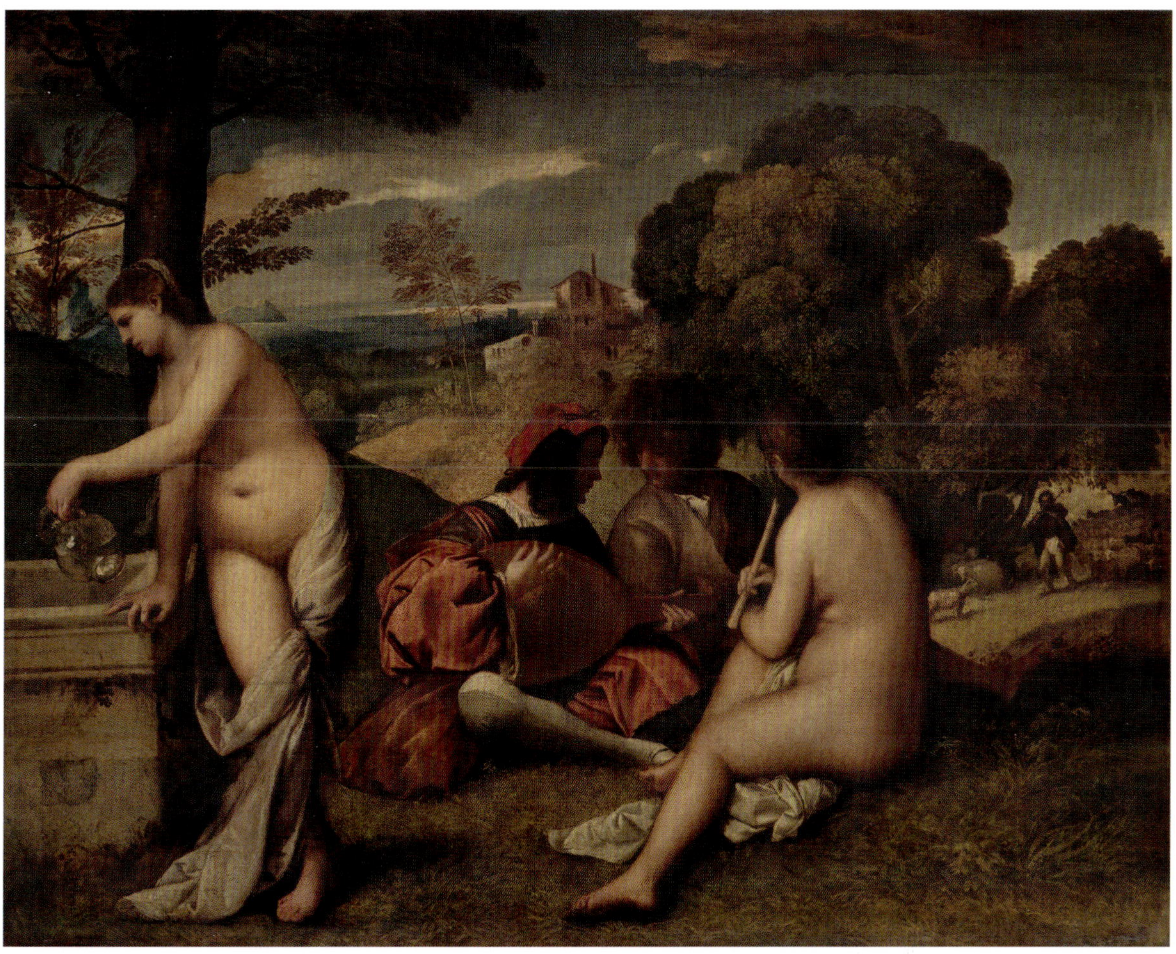

Fig. 16
Titian (Tiziano Vecellio)
The Pastoral Concert, ca. 1510
Oil on canvas
$41\frac{5}{16} \times 53\frac{15}{16}$ in.
(105 × 137 cm)
Musée du Louvre, Paris

portrait. However, the man in *The Pastoral Concert* is clearly a different person (if this was ever intended to be a real person). He is dressed differently—he and his hat, though red, are not the same. Even if the transfer between narrative painting and portraiture were so direct (and the history of the portrait as a genre seems to contradict this assumption), the approach to composition, light, shadow, volume, and drapery in *The Pastoral Concert* does not compare at all with the portrait at the Frick.[91]

The portrait in Frankfurt is a small panel retaining its original format of about six by seven inches, usually dated 1516. This dating is based on a label on the back of the painting that states, in old German, that the painting cost 15 ducats in 1516. Contrary to the usual dating in the literature, the

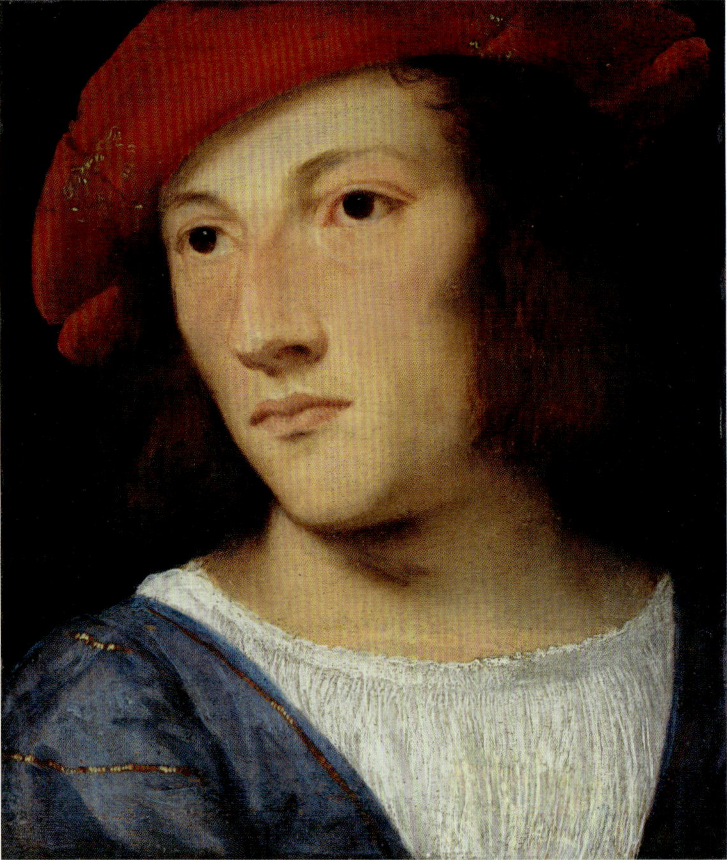

Fig. 17
Attributed to Titian (Tiziano Vecellio)
Portrait of a Youth, before 1516
Oil on panel (poplar)
7⅞ × 6¹¹⁄₁₆ in. (20 × 17 cm)
Städel Museum, Frankfurt

Fig. 18
Titian (Tiziano Vecellio)
Portrait of a Man with a Glove, ca. 1520
Oil on canvas
39⅜ × 35¹⁄₁₆ in. (100 × 89 cm)
Musée du Louvre, Paris

inscription implies that the panel was painted *before* 1516.[92] But how long before? Both stylistically and in terms of format, the portrait in Frankfurt is much closer to small portraits such as Giorgione's in San Diego (see fig. 9) than it is to the *Man in a Red Hat*.[93] Also, the attribution to Titian, though widely accepted, is far from evident. The propensity of experts to ascribe the panel to Titian recalls Charles Hope's remark that "scholars . . . have almost invariably taken it as an article of faith that the only young painters of real note working in Venice at this period were Giorgione, Titian, and Sebastiano because these were the ones mentioned by Vasari."[94]

Assuming that Titian's works followed a consistent stylistic development—which is not at all certain but is an inevitable precondition of connoisseurial dating of pictures about which nothing is known—there is one element in the Frick portrait that anchors it to the earliest phase of Titian's known career: the

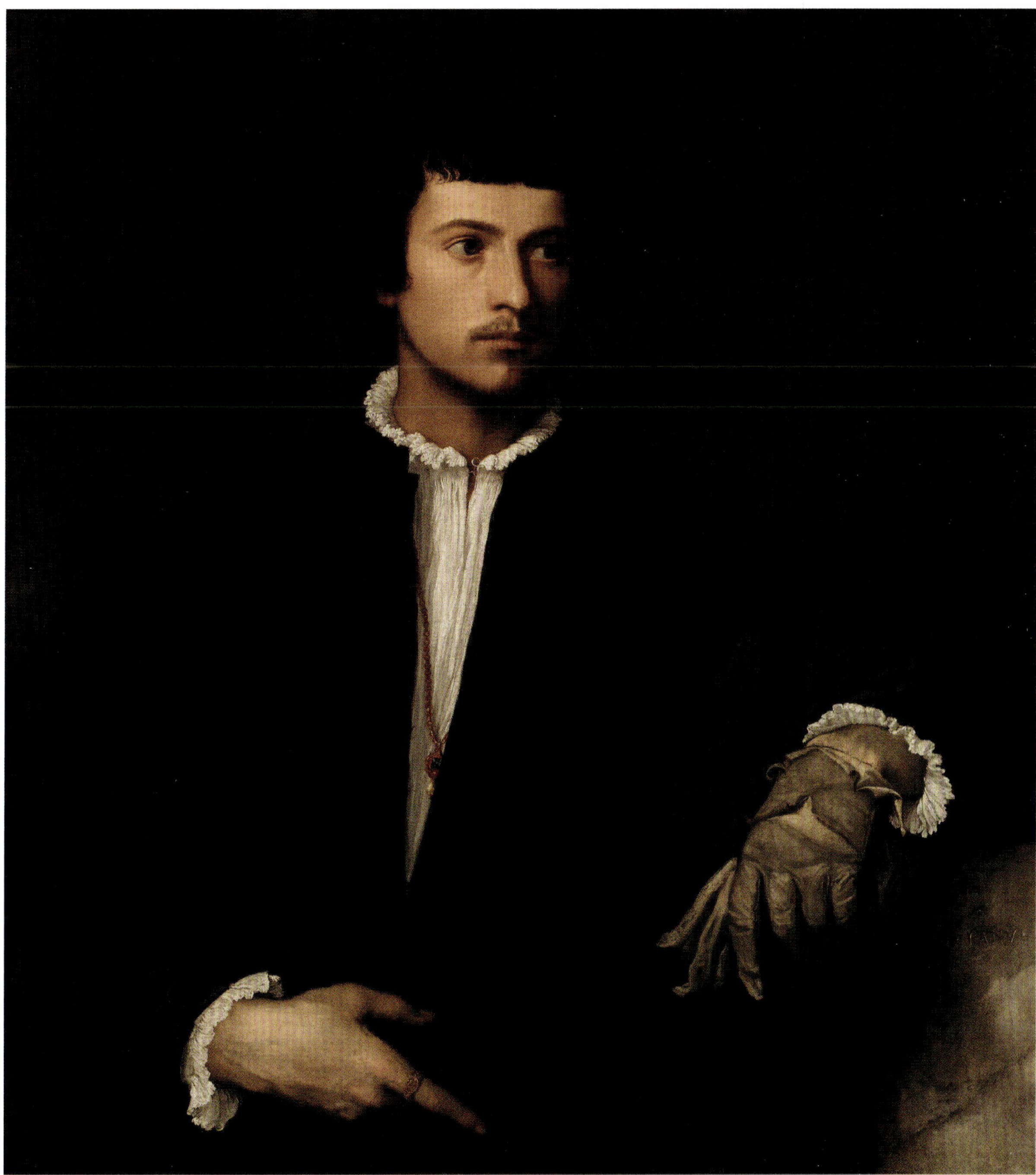

Fig. 19
Titian (Tiziano Vecellio)
Portrait of a Young Man, ca. 1520
Oil on canvas mounted on wood
35 3/16 × 29 1/4 in. (89.3 × 74.3 cm)
Alte Pinakothek, Munich

parapet. Problematized in poetry as images occupying a threshold between absence and presence, portraits of the fifteenth and early sixteenth centuries often materialize this threshold by means of a parapet.[95] While serving as a spatial locator and often a locus for communication with the viewer (think of *cartellini* attached to it), the parapet articulates a spatial and temporal bridge as much as a divide between here and there. In other words, they are far from negligible details. Nonetheless, toward the late 1510s, painters started to dispense with them in order to avoid any interruption between the space of the sitter and that of the viewer.

When inspected closely, the alleged parapet of the Frick portrait reveals itself as a shoddy line of gray paint and not much of a parapet at all. A simple comparison with *Gerolamo (?) Barbarigo* (see fig. 15) illustrates the point. The parapets in Titian's youthful pictures are painted as three-dimensional slabs of stone, sometimes inscribed, whose lighting is subtly orchestrated, and with which the sitters interact in one way or another.[96] The "parapet" in the Frick painting is nothing but a brushstroke. Unpublished conservation reports by William Suhr from 1974 reveal that the so-called parapet is indeed "a demarcation line" or a layer of paint to protect the canvas on the underside of the stretcher.[97] According to Arthur Grenfell's son, the painting was cleaned and relined after Hugh Lane bought it in 1906 and before it was sold to Grenfell in 1911.[98] X-rays now confirm that the original canvas rests in its entirety over a larger lining canvas, for which a new stretcher would have been required. All the margins of the canvas once nailed to the sides of the original stretcher, including the alleged "parapet," are now exposed as part of the picture field and repainted accordingly. With the new stretcher came the painting's current frame, which can already be seen in the photograph taken at Grenfell's Roehampton House in London (see fig. 7).

Brought back to its original format, the *Man in a Red Hat* is grander still. Compared to the portrait in the National Gallery in London (see fig. 15), the Frick painting appears to belong elsewhere stylistically. The main aspect that the Frick portrait seems to share with the paintings in London is some harshness in the delineation of the contours of the face, which can be traced to Titian's youthful fascination with Dürer's sharp lines. But its imposing full-frontal figure, the vagueness of the sitter's gaze, the balance of darkness and light in the background, and the looseness of the brushstrokes applied to the clothing do not find an equivalent in the London picture.

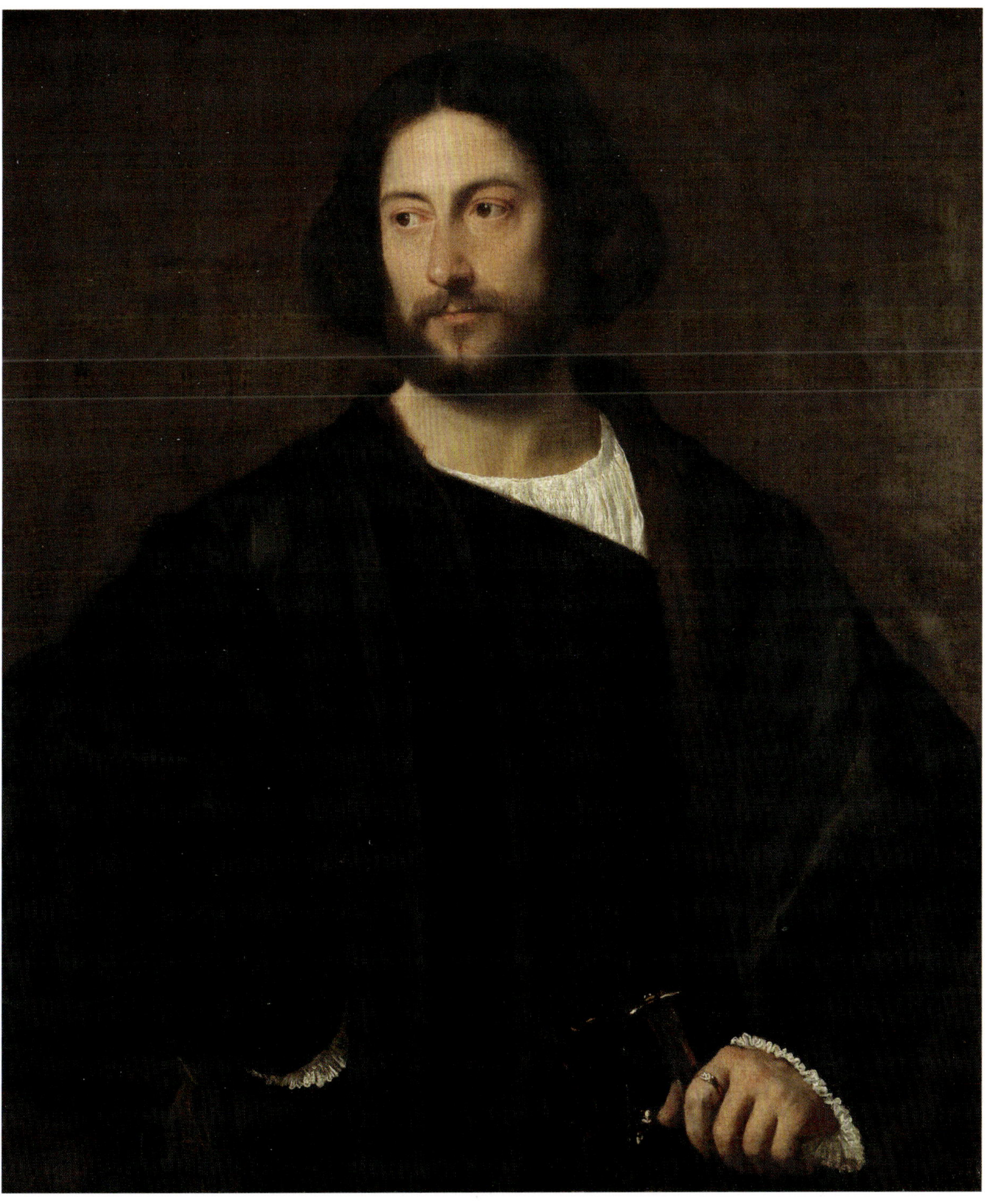

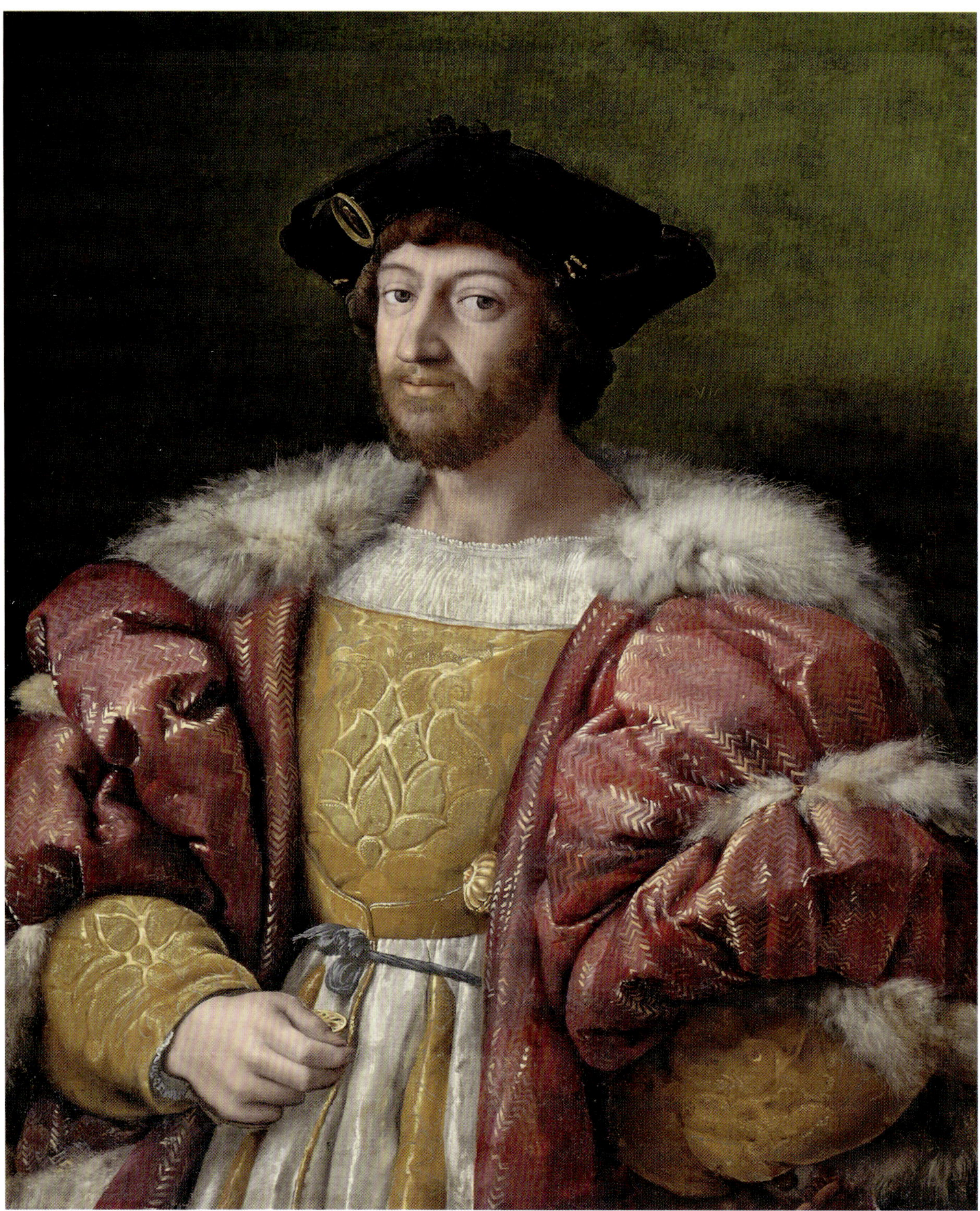

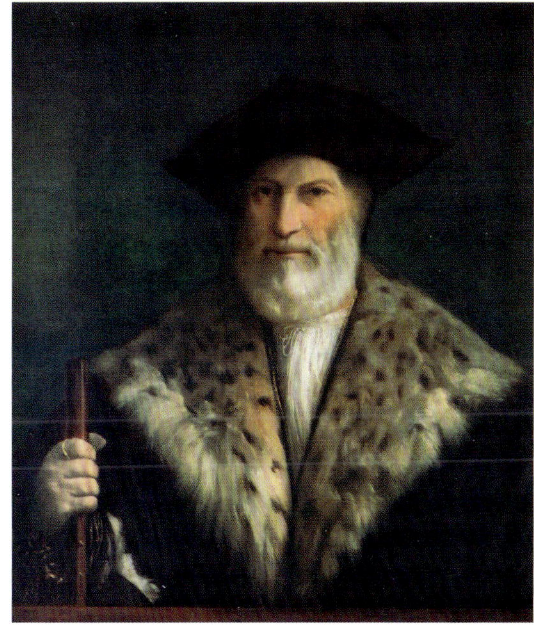

Instead, a comparison with portraits from a few years later, usually dated toward the end of the 1510s and the beginning of the 1520s, such as the *Portrait of a Man with a Glove* in Paris (fig. 18) or the portrait of an unidentified sitter in Munich (fig. 19), demonstrates their compositional and stylistic consistency.[99] Similarly poised, these sitters turn their gaze away from the viewer. In the absence of the parapet, their shoulders extend across the picture plane, almost as if to draw its space together. Despite the solidity of their pyramidal shape, they turn fluidly in space.[100] In all these portraits, the hands, previously hidden as much as possible, have come to be "made use of as an essential characteristic of the personality."[101] Advancing in the foreground, they carry objects laden with communicative potential: a golden ring, a sword, a book, or a pair of gloves. In the case of this last object, the exact same pair appears in the portrait at the Louvre (see fig. 18) as in the one at the Frick.

Examining the possibility that the *Man in a Red Hat* dates from the second half of the 1510s, it seems likely that it occupies a key position in relation to Raphael's contemporary achievements in the field of portraiture, as encapsulated in his *Lorenzo de' Medici* (fig. 20).[102] Between 1516 and 1519, while Titian was painting a series of large canvases for the *camerini* (little rooms) of Duke Alfonso I d'Este in Ferrara, the duke was trying relentlessly to obtain paintings by Raphael but to no avail because the painter was then working ceaselessly in the Vatican *stanze*.[103] Until his sudden death in 1520, Raphael had the habit of sending drawings and cartoons to Alfonso to appease him.[104] If underwhelming for Alfonso, these Raphaelesque materials must have caused some excitement among the painters at his court, among them Dosso Dossi (1489–1542), with whom Titian had begun a fruitful exchange. Presumably, the two artists, who took a trip together to the court of Mantua in 1519, became quite close.[105] It is in dialogue with Raphael's *Lorenzo de' Medici* (once believed to be the sitter of the Frick portrait) that Dosso's *Portrait of an Elderly Man in a Fur* in Milan (fig. 21) or the *Portrait of a Man* at the Louvre (fig. 22) find their place next to

Fig. 20
Raphael (Raffaello Sanzio)
Lorenzo de' Medici, Duke of Urbino, 1518
Oil on canvas
38 × 31 in. (97 × 79 cm)
Private collection

Fig. 21
Dosso Dossi (Giovanni Luteri)
Portrait of an Elderly Man in a Fur, ca. 1518–21
Oil on canvas
28⅜ × 26 in. (72 × 66 cm)
Saibene Collection, Milan

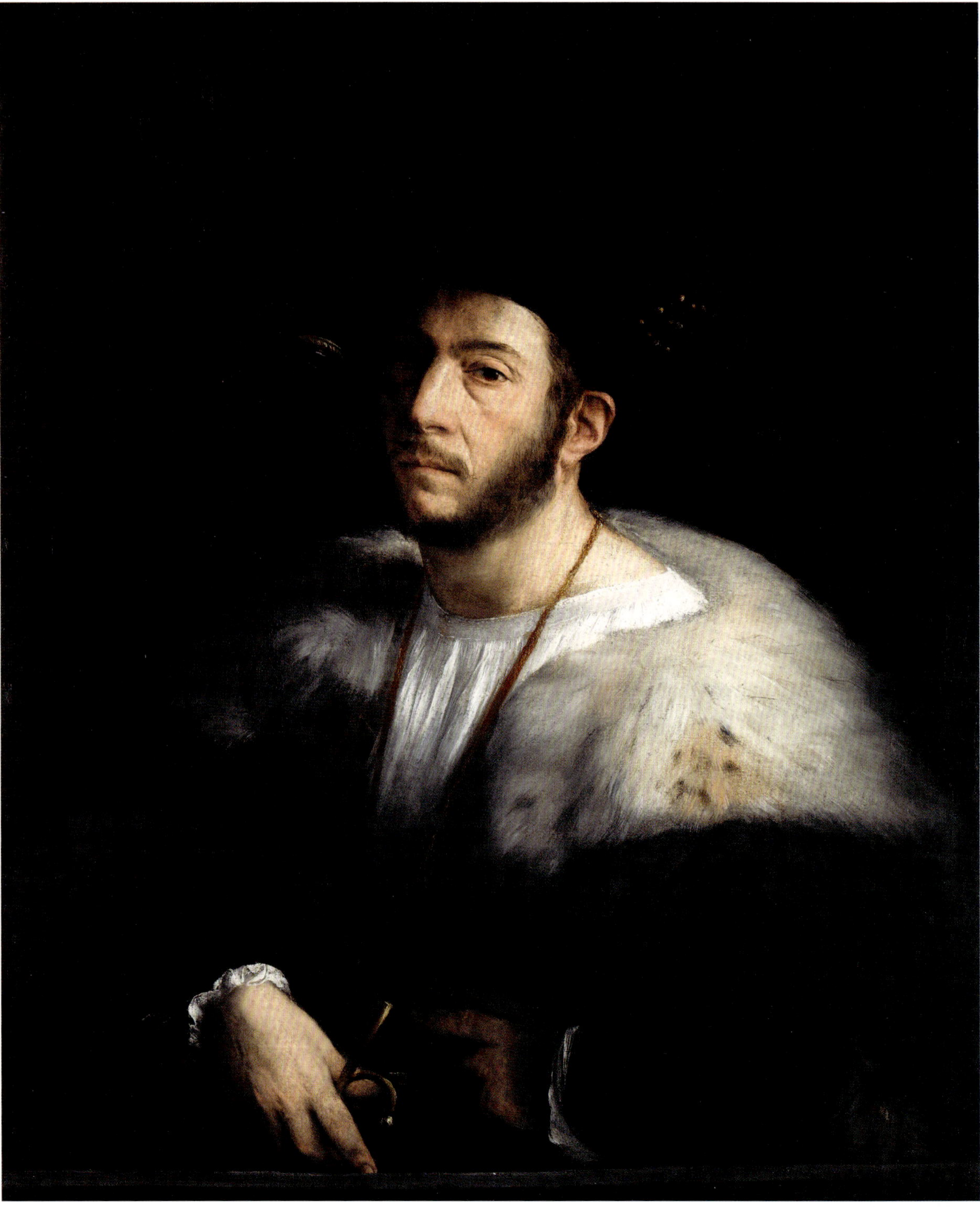

Titian's *Man in a Red Hat.*[106] Here, one finds the same attention to the texture of the fur as in Dosso's paintings; the same reddish undertones; the same brilliance of the paint; the same monumental presence of the body; and the same golden light permeating the painting, an element that does not occur in subsequent portraits by Titian.

Building on elements both internal and external to Titian's oeuvre, the painting seems to be an exquisite example of the artist's portraiture in the second half of the 1510s. Working as a link between the portraiture of the early 1510s and that of the early 1520s, the painting at the Frick seems to blend "Giorgionesque" portraiture with formal innovations characteristic of the papal court of Rome, as known to Titian mostly through the mediation of the Ferrarese court of Alfonso I.[107] Arguably, this dating is corroborated by historical evidence around the clothing of the figure.

Clothing, Status, and Identity

The large red hat worn by the sitter of Titian's portrait at the Frick is so distinctive that the portrait is usually titled after it (although for a long time the hat was imprecisely termed a "cap"). Presumably velvet, the hat is held together by black drawstrings terminating in a tassel that can be seen on the right. Lined in lynx fur, the black velvet outer garment—a so-called *vesta* or a *zupon*—points to the sitter's affluence.[108] Underneath the outer garment is a gold-thread brocade *saione*, with a black velvet band—a garment that would extend halfway down the thighs—under which is a simple white shirt (*camicia*). This young dandy is also wearing slashed leather gloves, which normally would have been softened and perfumed with scents such as cedar oil, milk, or even brandy.[109] Lastly, he holds in his left hand the cruciform hilt of a sword, of a type that is hard to identify. Based on its shape, it is likely a rapier, a thirty-inch-long sidearm normally worn in civilian dress.[110] Overall, this is an exceedingly lavish costume, befitting a very rich and possibly aristocratic sitter.

The dating of pictures through clothing is riddled with difficulties and often involves circular arguments. The dating of such clothing is based on other paintings, which are themselves dated mostly through their style. Also, fashion changes according to time but also to place. Making things even more difficult, Italian courtiers of the Cinquecento enjoyed dressing in foreign costumes, as stated by Castiglione in his *Cortegiano*:

Fig. 22
Dosso Dossi (Giovanni Luteri)
Portrait of a Man, ca. 1518
Oil on canvas
37⅜ × 30 5⁄16 in. (95 × 77 cm)
Musée du Louvre, Paris

Following pages:

Fig. 23
Bartolomeo Veneto
Portrait of a Man, 1520
Oil on panel
27⅞ × 20½ in. (70.8 × 52.1 cm)
The Museum of Fine Arts, Houston

Fig. 24
Michel Sittow
Diego de Guevara (?), ca. 1515–18
Oil on panel
13½ × 9 15⁄16 in. (33.6 × 23.7 cm)
National Gallery of Art, Washington

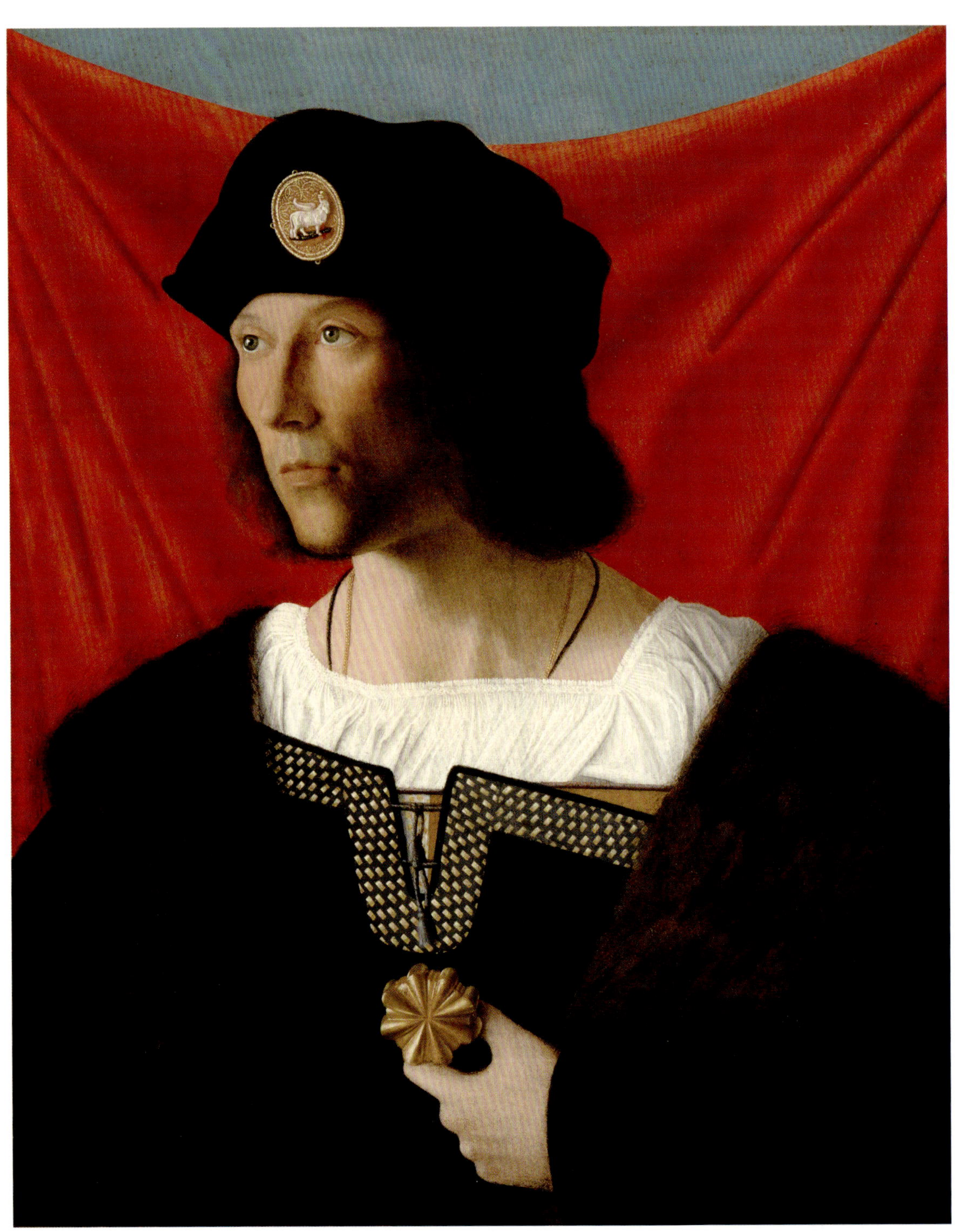

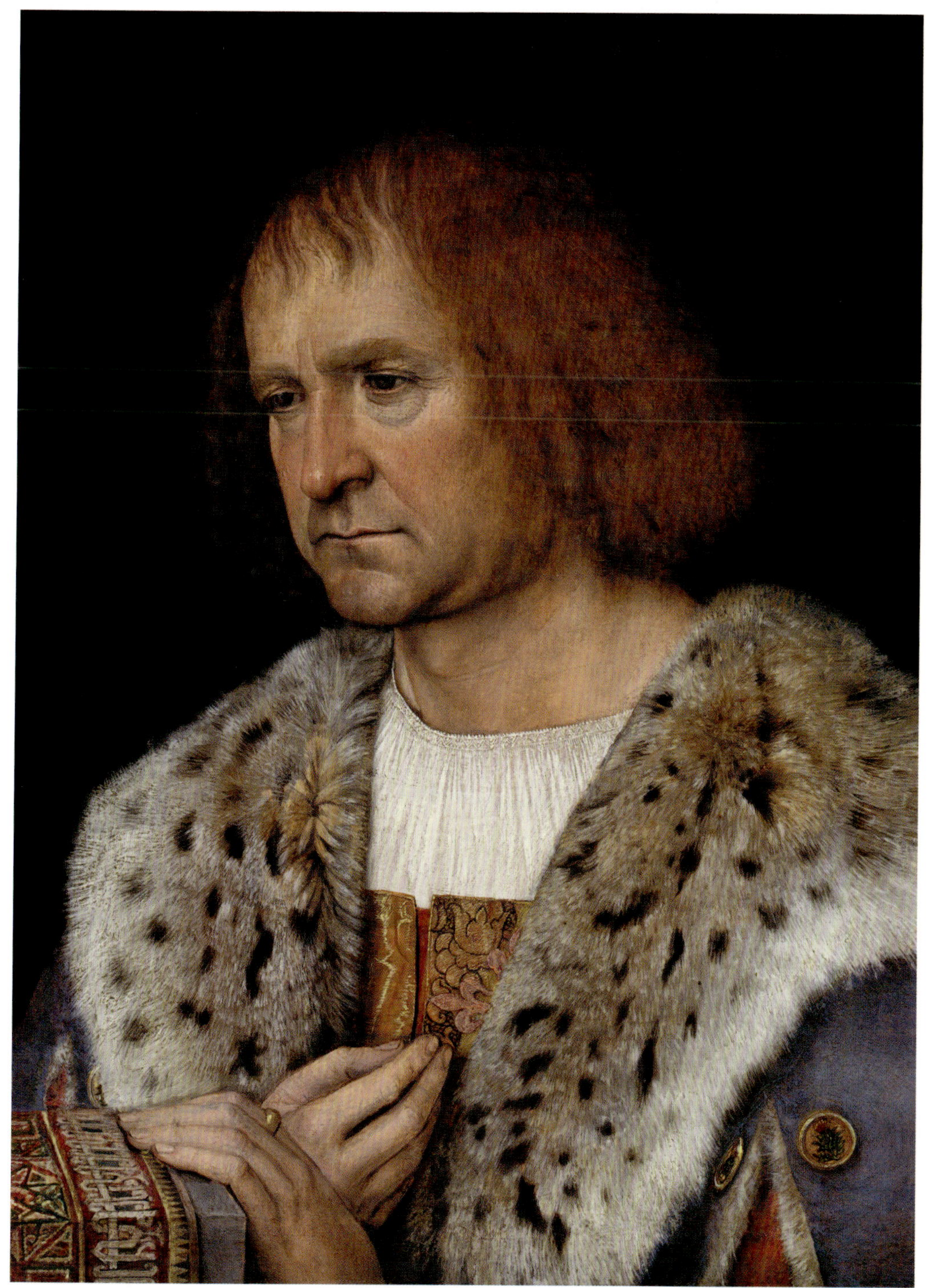

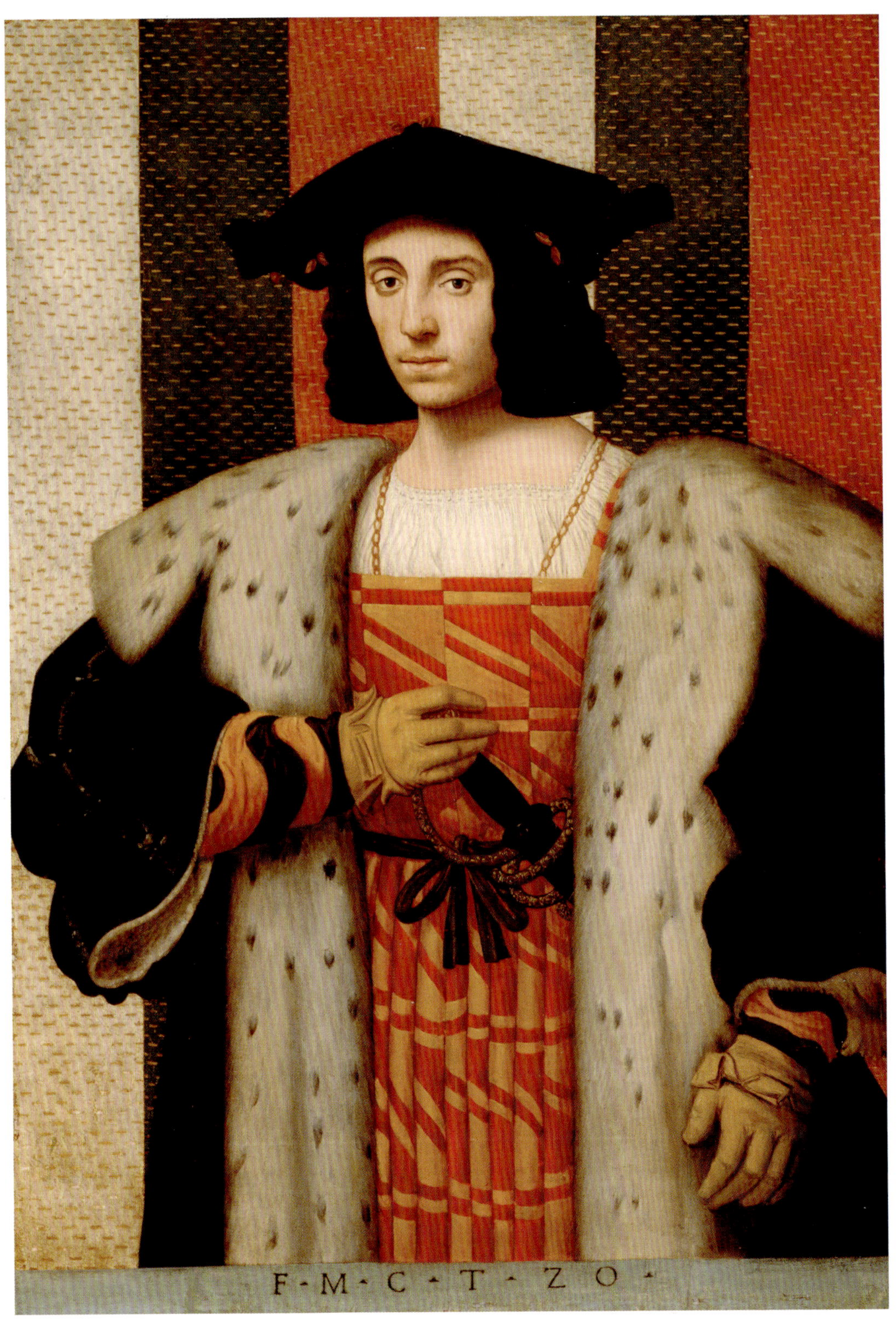
F · M · C · T · ZO ·

> [Giuliano de' Medici:] "In this we see an infinite variety: some dressing after the French manner, some after the Spanish, some wishing to appear German; nor are those lacking who dress in the style of Turks; some wear beards, some not. It would therefore be well to know how to choose the best out of this confusion." Messer Federico [Fregoso] replied: "I do not really know how to give an exact rule about dress, except that a man ought to follow the custom of the majority; and since, just as you say, that custom is so varied, and the Italians are so fond of dressing in the style of other peoples, I think that everyone should be permitted to dress as he pleases."[111]

Fig. 25
Bernardino de' Conti
Gentleman of the Trivulzio Family (?), possibly 1520
Oil on panel, 42¹⁵⁄₁₆ × 29⅞ × ¹¹⁄₁₆ in. (109 × 74 × 1.8 cm)
Detroit Institute of Arts

So, although there may seem to be something distinctly French about the costume of the *Man in a Red Hat*, it is far from certain that the sitter is a Frenchman. In fact, since he does not wear the fringe so characteristic of contemporary French hairstyle, he is much more likely to be Italian.[112]

All precautions notwithstanding, several costume comparisons tie the *Man in a Red Hat* to the second half of the 1510s—first, with a portrait by Bartolomeo Veneto now in Houston, dated 1520 (fig. 23),[113] and second, should the sitter not be Italian, with Michel Sittow's possible portrait of Diego de Guevara, also dated to the second half of the 1510s (fig. 24).[114] But the most compelling comparison of all is with Bernardino de' Conti's alleged portrait of Giovan Francesco Trivulzio, also dated about 1520 (fig. 25).[115] Here, despite the difference in format and quality, the sitter wears the same type of haircut, the same gloves, the same kind of lynx-lined cloak worn over a gold-thread *saione*, and even holds the sword in a similar way. Despite the difference in format, the similarity is so striking that one may think that Bernardino knew Titian's portrait and referenced it compositionally. The comparison with the Bernardino's portrait, more overtly heraldic, also helps to position the sitter of the Frick portrait socially.

Somehow, though, the comparison with Bernardino de' Conti's stiff portrait also helps us to realize that Titian's portrait accommodates some tension between opposing aspirations. Unlike Trivulzio, Titian's moonstruck sitter seems not to be a military man—or, at least, seems not to wish to be described as such in the portrait.[116] Held up nonchalantly with the left hand, the sword—the only functional object in this attribute-less portrait—just so happens to be there, as if belonging to our "Hamlet of the Lagoons" not by will but almost by birthright, as is also the case for Lorenzo de' Medici in the portrait by Raphael (see fig. 20).

Fig. 26
Titian (Tiziano Vecellio)
Federico II Gonzaga, Marquess of Mantua, late 1520s (?)
Oil on panel
49³⁄₁₆ × 39 in. (125 × 99 cm)
Museo del Prado, Madrid

However frequently swords may appear in portraits of the early Cinquecento in Italy, scholars have never pointed out that only little more than twenty of almost one hundred portraits of male sitters by Titian flaunt a sword. More important, with the exception of a couple of sitters as yet unidentified, the men carrying swords in Titian portraits all belong to the highest ranks of the Italian (and European) sixteenth-century aristocracy: emperors and kings, viceroys, heads of state, and offspring of princely families. Among them, only one seems to be Venetian—Gabriele Tadino, who ranked high among the republic's military forces.[117] This comes as no surprise because it was strictly forbidden to carry a sword in the streets of Venice.[118] Although such strict rules probably existed precisely because they were largely ignored, it seems likely that Venetian patricians would still deem it inappropriate to be portrayed with a sword by their side. One may object that, as Giovan Paolo Lomazzo put it in his *Trattato dell'arte della pittura* (1584), "the merchants and bankers, who never saw an unsheathed sword, whom one would expect to see with a pen behind their ear, shrouded in their gown [*gonella*], their notebook before them, instead have themselves portrayed in full suit of armor, holding batons like those of generals—which is a most ridiculous thing."[119] However, as Johannes Wilde pointed out, this seems to be a much later phenomenon—a "bourgeois tendency" emerging at least after the Sack of Rome (1527).[120]

The sitter of the Frick portrait must be an extremely high-ranking individual from a princely family—probably Italian, considering that at this stage Titian's fame had not yet extended beyond the Alps, and presumably no foreign candidate of such distinction would call upon an (as yet) little-known painter. However, one candidate who was then within Titian's reach was Federico II Gonzaga (1500–1540), the first-born son of Isabella d'Este and Francesco II, Marquess of Mantua.[121]

When the portrait was painted, about 1516–19, Federico would have been sixteen to nineteen years old, an age that aligns quite well with the sitter's pubescent beard.[122] Federico had brown eyes, like the sitter, and was often celebrated as the handsomest young prince of his time. Aged ten to thirteen, Federico had been part of Pope Julius II's court in Rome, where he was forced to reside as a hostage in exchange for the liberation of his father from Venetian custody. Soon thereafter, he spent another three years as a hostage at the court of King Francis I of France. At the French court, he developed a taste for expensive clothing, encouraged by his mother, who understood that he could

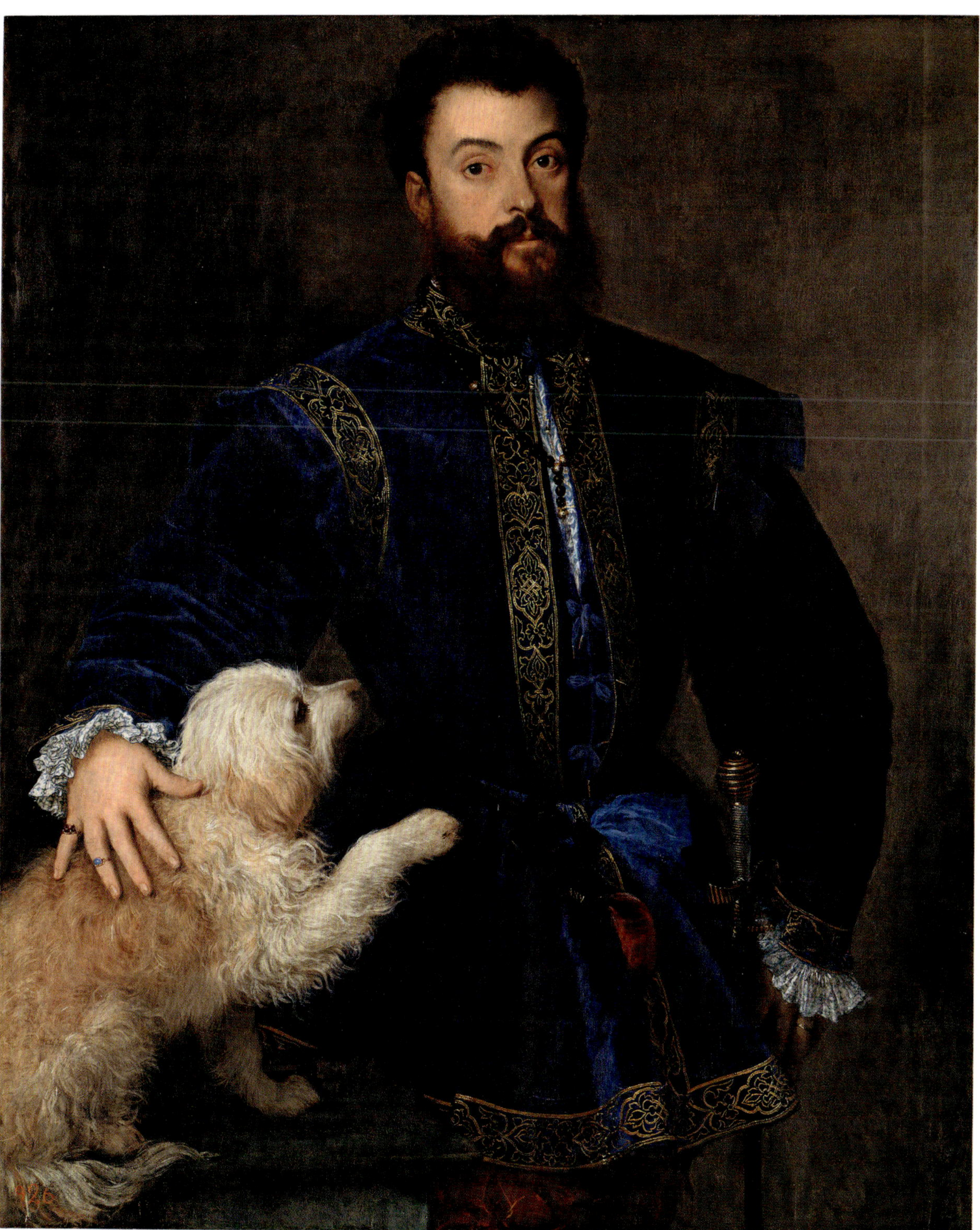

Fig. 27
Titian (Tiziano Vecellio)
Francesco Maria della Rovere, Duke of Urbino, ca. 1537
Oil on canvas
44⅞ × 40⁹⁄₁₆ in. (114 × 103 cm)
Gallerie degli Uffizi, Florence

be used as a gorgeous pawn on her political chessboard.[123] Although engaging in the military activities that came with his title, Federico was equally interested in the arts as he was in lovemaking and poetry.[124] In May 1517, his parents sent him an expensive golden vest with which to return triumphantly to Italy.[125] Soon after his homebound journey, Federico left on a trip to Venice (where he also went in 1520). Upon his arrival there, Marin Sanudo, the Venetian chronicler, records that he was dressed in a way strikingly similar to the sitter in Titian's portrait at the Frick:

> His Lordship [Federico] was well dressed, with a gold-and-white robe [*sajon*] and, over it, a black velvet vest [*zupon*] and a velvet beret on his head.[126]

It is worth adding that Mantuan rulers were famous for what may be termed a "sartorial diplomacy" conducted via headwear and gloves, both of which play a crucial role in the Frick portrait.[127] Even if we cannot be certain of the sitter's identity, these data, as well as Sanudo's description, serve to substantiate the social standing of the sitter, as well as the chronology of the Frick portrait.

During the following years, Federico, who succeeded his father in 1519, became one of Titian's most devoted patrons. His later portrait (fig. 26) reveals his sophisticated conception of what a "state portrait" should look like, especially when compared to the portrait of his brother-in-law, Francesco Maria I della Rovere, Duke of Urbino, also by Titian (fig. 27).[128] It is clear that Federico's self-fashioning was not predicated on his military ambition, signaled modestly by the sword on his left. Though less gaunt, his likeness here is not far from that of the sitter in the Frick portrait. Admittedly, the beard obscures much of the lineaments of the face, but the eyes, nose, and mouth appear to be very similar. As to the hair, documents reveal that in France he had kept it long.[129] Additionally, in the earliest portrait of him, made by Francesco Francia in 1510 (fig. 28), his hair does verge toward ginger, and he has a cleft chin much like that of the sitter in the Frick portrait.[130]

As to the circumstances of Federico's meeting with Titian, it is important to remember that Federico's sojourn in Venice in 1517 occurred at the same time that Titian was working on the canvases for Alfonso's *camerini* in Ferrara, which Federico visited that same month and also the following year.[131] It seems probable that their paths crossed over this period of time. Indeed, although scholars date the origins of their relationship to 1523, a fresh reading of

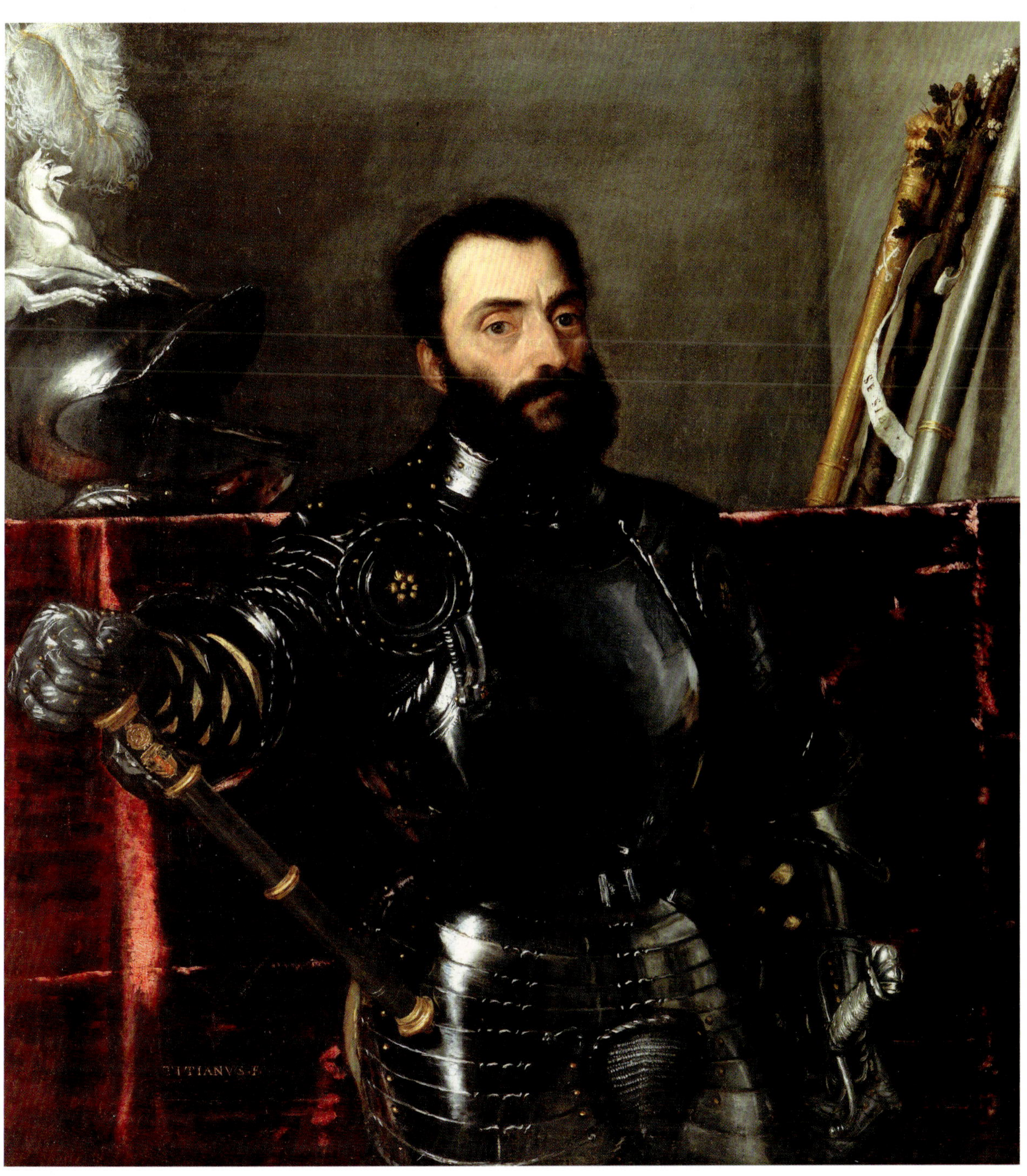
TITIANVS.F.

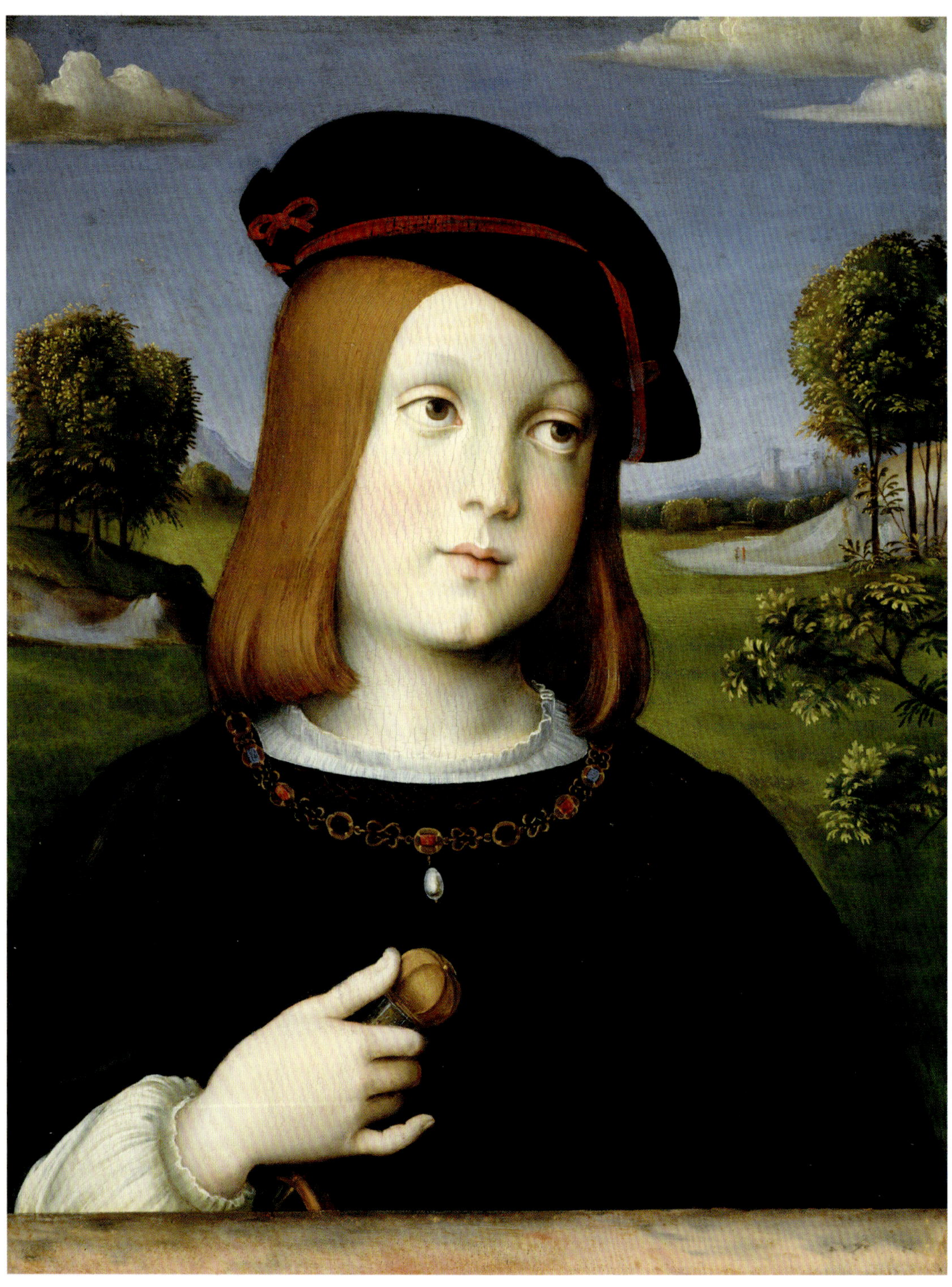

documentary evidence suggests that such a relationship was ongoing as early as 1519.[132] A letter by Girolamo da Sestola to Isabella d'Este reports that when Titian and Dosso went on their Mantuan trip in 1519, they "saw the things by Mantegna . . . and praised your study rooms"—the innermost rooms of the Ducal Palace, which they had accessed unbeknownst to Isabella.[133] This suggests that Federico, having recently succeeded his father, had granted the painters such a privilege. Indeed, another letter of December 1522 contains an order issued by Federico to his Venetian agent Gian Battista Malatesta:

Fig. 28
Francesco Francia (Francesco Raibolini)
Federico II Gonzaga as a Young Boy, 1510
Tempera on wood, transferred from wood to canvas and then again to wood
18⅞ × 14 in. (47.9 × 35.6 cm)
The Metropolitan Museum of Art, New York; Benjamin Altman Bequest

> We want you to invite *maestro* Titian the painter to come and stay here with us for the holidays for eight or ten days, praying him to do so for our sake, for he will be most welcome and we will be glad to see him.[134]

This friendly invitation to spend the holidays together suggests that artist and patron had known each other for a long time before a Gonzaga commission of a painting from Titian is first mentioned in a letter from Alfonso to Federico in 1523.[135]

Unfortunately, all surviving works made by Titian for the Gonzagas—including the Prado portrait (see fig. 26), usually dated 1529 despite a lack of evidence[136]—are impossible to date with precision or to locate in surviving inventories of the family's possessions.[137] The same applies to the Frick portrait: if it was ever intended to be a portrait of Federico, no documentation survives connecting it to the family. Though enticing, the hypothesis remains speculative.

Ideal Portraits and Male Beauty

Over the past decades, scholars have shown how the painting of people was "a heady realm of experimentation" in Cinquecento Italy.[138] While Titian's portraits are naturalistic in their details, they are also marked by a distinctive and unhesitating personal style. The resulting combination of artifice and candor, as well as the importance given to presentation as opposed to strict verisimilitude by both the sitter and their painter, makes portraits such as Titian's *Man in a Red Hat* more complex than they would first appear. A simplified way of thinking about these works is presented in a letter of January 26, 1960, from the art historian Florence Kossoff to Franklin Biebel, then director of the Frick:

Fig. 29
Titian (Tiziano Vecellio)
Portrait of a Woman ("La Bella"), 1536–38
Oil on canvas
35 1/16 × 29 3/4 in. (89 × 75.5 cm)
Galleria Palatina, Palazzo Pitti, Florence

> I'm beginning to wonder if most of these Venetian portraits of the early 16th century are meant to be representations of specific people or if they couldn't simply represent a particular type of physiognomy and personality.[139]

Theories such as this have gained some currency in parallel to Elizabeth Cropper's studies of Cinquecento portraits of *belle donne* (beautiful women).[140] In Cropper's compelling reconstruction, many sixteenth-century paintings of "beautiful women" conformed visually to conventions for the description of beautiful women in poetry. In the context of a society that valued a hierarchical conception of the arts, and against the backdrop of the so-called *paragone* (comparison, or competition) between poetry and painting, Cropper argues that by giving visual representation to poetic conventions used to describe women in verse, early sixteenth-century portraits of beautiful women proved that painting could describe Beauty as much as poetry did—thereby elevating the status of painting among the arts. In Cropper's reconstruction, many portraits of unknown beautiful women should be characterized as representations of ideal beauty in which the question of identity is immaterial. Titian's portrait of an unknown woman popularly known as *La Bella* (the beautiful) (fig. 29) is one among many cases validating Cropper's theory. Writing to Titian to organize delivery of this work, Duke Francesco Maria I della Rovere referred to it as "that portrait of the woman wearing the blue dress."[141] However much the likeness of *La Bella* was drawn after a real model, her identity was inconsequential for the duke.

If such ideal portraits existed for women, why not posit their existence for men too? The reason is simple: with few exceptions, Italian poetry of the time was dedicated exclusively to women. If portraits of ideal beauties were produced in order to participate in the debate as to the superiority of painting over poetry, such debate was bound to the canon of Petrarchan poetry, which was directed exclusively at women.[142] What is more, the cultural codes for the vernacular celebration of male beauty in Cinquecento Italy were not yet so fixed as to offer a series of characteristics that encouraged imitation and admiration. In other words, vernacular Italian—this relatively new language—had not yet forged the tools to characterize ideal male beauty, neither in poetry nor in painting. Nor had it any interest in doing so yet.[143]

Unlike Petrarchan poetry, the antique—both visual and poetic—did offer a repertoire for the idealization of male, not just female, beauty. A

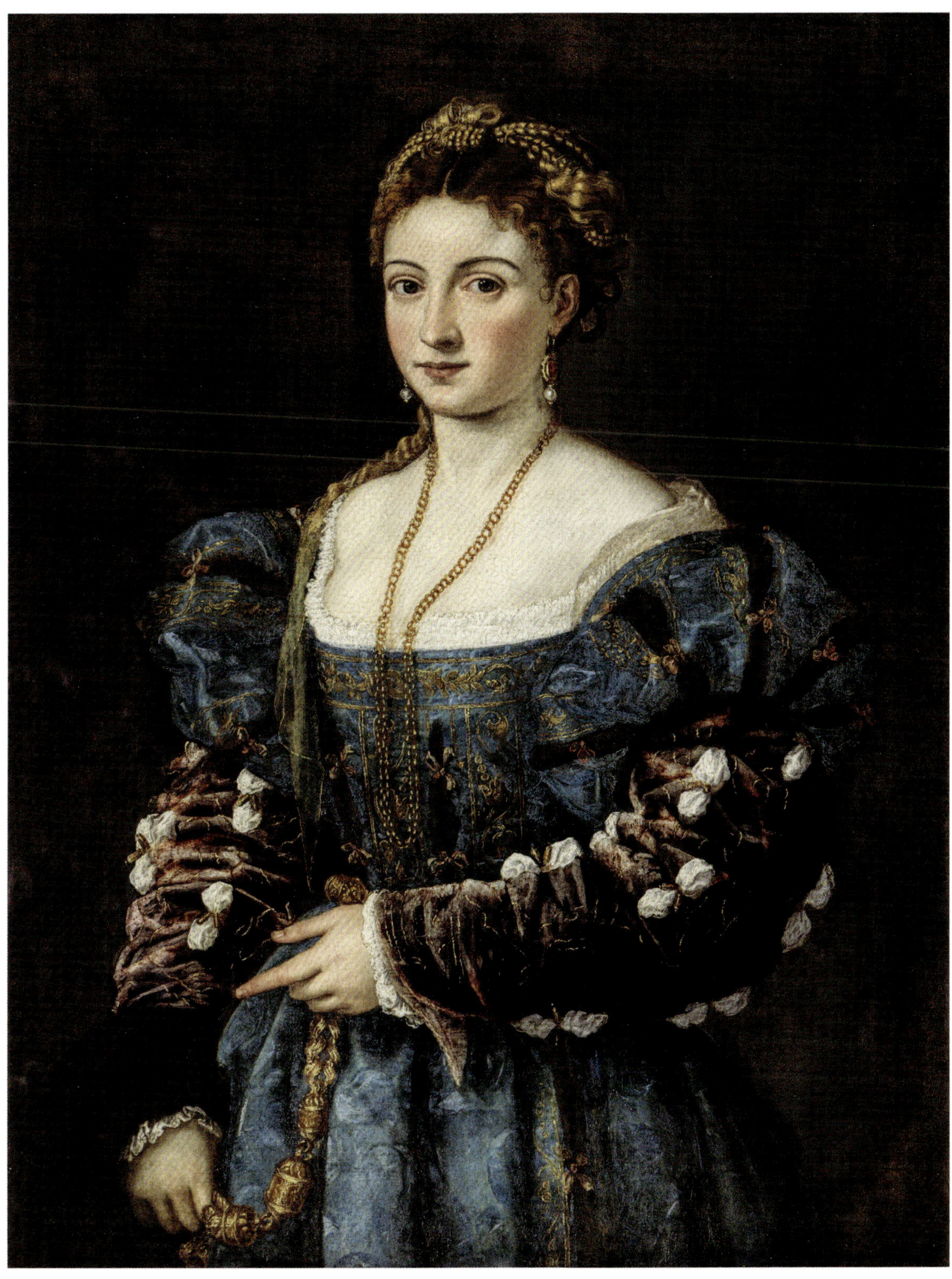

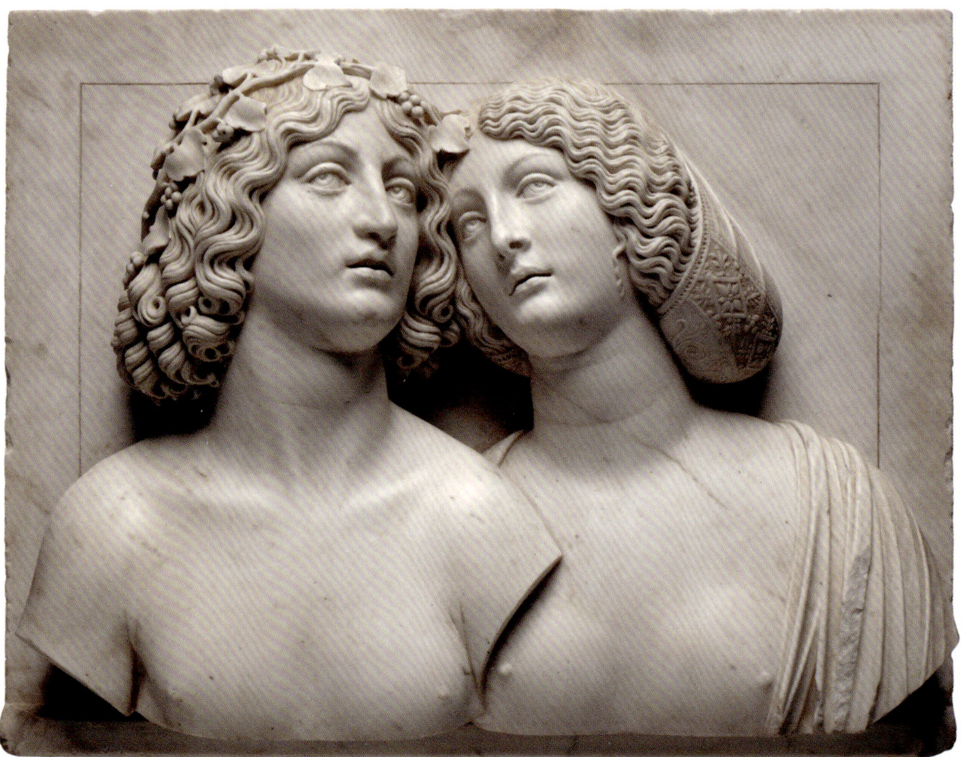

Fig. 30
Tullio Lombardo
Young Couple, ca. 1505–10
Marble with traces of polychromy
22 1/16 × 27 15/16 × 7 7/8 in.
(56 × 71 × 20 cm)
Kunsthistorisches Museum, Vienna

suitable example may be the famous couple by Tullio Lombardo (fig. 30).[144] But here, if the question of the identity of male *and* female sitters in works such as this was indeed irrelevant, that was because such sitters pursued the translation of their likeness into works that could be taken as antiques, as relics of an ancient, unknowable past. In other words, the point of classicizing portraiture was less ideal beauty (and the competition with poetry) than it was the cult of antiquity. On the contrary, there was no possibility of modern, early sixteenth-century portraits of a male sitter being idealized in the vernacular, either visual or literary. No unidentified male portrait of the Cinquecento can be said to be a beautiful representation made for its own sake. To see Titian's *Portrait of a Man in a Red Hat* as a portrait of ideal male beauty is to read it, if inadvertently, through the lens of romanticism. This is not to deny that contemporary viewers may have perceived a male sitter as beautiful nor that his representation might become an object of desire.[145] Quite the contrary. For the male Erotic, unlike the male Beautiful, was very much within the possibilities of vernacular painting.[146]

"My Favorite Renaissance Sex Object"

A good friend of Titian's, Daniele Barbaro, once prescribed how a good painter should paint:

> [One ought to] paint the contours with sweetness and *sfumato*, so that you can understand even that which is not there, instead of making the eye believe that it [only] sees what meets the eye, which [here] is a most sweet fugue, a tenderness in the horizon of our sight, something which is, yet isn't—and one can achieve this only with infinite practice.[147]

Approaching the *Man in a Red Hat* at close range, one can still see the gold of the *saione* extending under the fur above the sitter's left hand. Similarly, an originally larger profile for the hat has left a red aura surrounding the sitter's head. Titian's pentimenti are left visible, and so is his every brushstroke. In the large spans of black, apparently providing an interval of rest to one's eyes, Titian plays with different levels of glossiness—a distinction that is lost even in the best reproductions.[148] The texture of the painting is further enriched by the grainy canvas, which catches light in its ridges and helps to articulate the structure of the beard. Involving the viewer in a haptic form of gaze, while also blurring the contours of the image, Titian's portrait prompts the viewer to feel "something which *is* yet *isn't*."[149] On a psychological level, the portrait also half encourages, half frustrates the viewer's attempt to comprehend the sitter's *moti dell'animo*: because these *moti* are never quite knowable, the beholder ends up projecting their own emotions onto the picture. Ultimately, the *moti dell'animo* present in the portrait are as much the receptive viewer's as they are the sitter's.

There is a great deal of tension in the suspended moment chosen by Titian for this portrait, which toys more than most with the boundaries between absence and presence. Stirring the viewer's emotions vis-à-vis the sitter's, while also exciting tactile imagination, a portrait like the *Man in a Red Hat* stimulates sensuality and desire. As Marianne Koos has pointed out, the work at the Frick is not too different in this regard from the many Venetian portraits of women whose robes slide over their shoulders, among which Titian's roughly contemporary *Flora* (fig. 31) represents in many ways a parallel to the *Man in a Red Hat*.[150] Like the man's left collarbone that comes into view from under the shirt as he turns, her left nipple is nearly exposed. As the viewer's gaze travels along the breasts of the woman, vibrant juxtapositions of

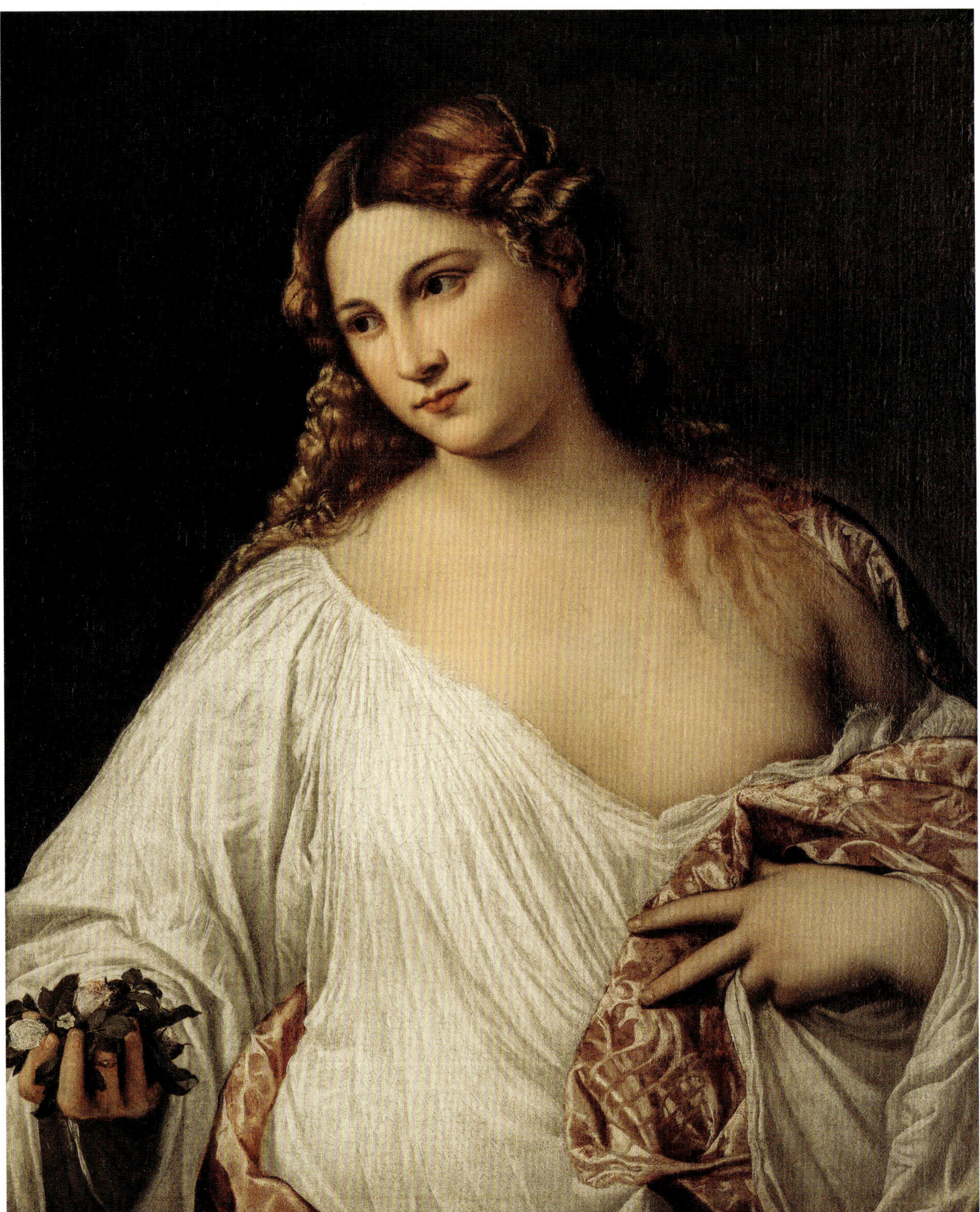

materials are deliberately arranged to arouse the audience's haptic sensitivity. The figure in the *Man in a Red Hat* may be more fully dressed, but he invites as much undressing. For the sensuality of these paintings lies in their tactile qualities more than the outward eroticism of the image; in their eyes and bodies, which—active, mobile, and willful—promise presence. As Germaine Greer put it ever so bluntly:

Fig. 31
Titian (Tiziano Vecellio)
Portrait of a Woman ("Flora"), ca. 1517
Oil on canvas
31⅜ × 24¹⁵⁄₁₆ in.
(79.7 × 63.5 cm)
Gallerie degli Uffizi, Florence

> My favourite Renaissance sex object is fully, even heavily dressed. He is not visible at all below the waist, so that the state of his sexual readiness is a mystery to the beholder. He wears a voluminous jacket with lappets of some luxurious fur, like lynx. On his left hand he wears a soft grey leather glove, with a slit at the back above the button, through which his skin glows like a pearl, and with that hand he draws through the lips of his coat the bulbous pommel of a rapier. The expression on his face is noncommittal, but his lips seem to quiver with the beginnings of something more significant than a smile. Perhaps he means to disarm and let his heavy coat slip to the floor; perhaps he does not. He is a Man in a Red Cap painted by Titian, and he hangs all day and every day in the Frick Museum in New York.[151]

Ultimately, in the *Man in a Red Hat*, Titian's procedure is exposed as a way of showing the painting's human subject "so that each infuses our sense of the other."[152] Like the handwriting in a letter from a friend, Titian's visible technique is a pledge of authorship but also of presence.[153] As William Hazlitt wrote in 1844, "Whenever you turn to look at Titian's portraits . . . there seems to be some question pending between you, as though an intimate friend or inveterate foe were in the room with you," which is why "most other pictures" may be left "hanging up in a collection," but—he reflects—Titian's portraits should always hang in one's house "for company."[154] It is only fitting that The Frick Collection happens to be a house, too.

Notes

1 Judd 2016, 75.

2 Ahearn 2003, 451, doc. 594.

3 The article continues: "It contained an excellent collection of old masters, which passed with the estate into the possession of Sir George Yonge, who married Cleeve's daughter. This collection was sold by auction by White at 4, Stratford-place, Oxford-street, on March 24 and 25, 1806, and this so-called Titian was presumably included in the sale, but it is not mentioned in the list of pictures at Foot's Cray Place published in the *English Connoisseur* (1767, 1: 57–62) nor yet in *Everyman's Magazine* of October 1772; so it may have been a later addition to the Cleeve collection"; *Times* 1906, 7.

4 *Times* 1911, 8.

5 Brockwell 1914a, 5.

6 *Times* 1914, 5.

7 Brockwell 1914b, 9.

8 *Connoisseur* 1914, 264–65. The same magazine had been following the history of the painting since 1911; *Connoisseur* 1911, 267.

9 *Catalogue* 1968, 2: 251–55 (esp. 255n.24). Letters exchanged among Lord Methuen, John Pope-Hennessy, Harry D. M. Grier, and Bernice Davidson illustrate the confusion surrounding the provenance; New York, The Frick Collection, Curatorial Department, Curatorial Files (cited hereafter as CF): 1915.1.116, Correspondence.

10 Christie, Manson & Woods, London, May 1–4, 1876 (lot 204, May 2).

11 Fischel 1924, 325; Woodward 1963.

12 "Una storietta del martirio di santo Andrea apostolo ebbe Paolo del Sera, poi Senatore fiorentino, che se la portò a Venezia: e fu una delle prime cose, che in quella città furono vedute di sua [i.e., Carlo Dolci's] mano. . . . Un'altra simile istoria condusse pel marchese Carlo Gerini, ed una eziandio per Carlo Corbinelli, posseduta oggi da Andrea del Rosso, gentiluomo . . . e tutte e tre l'istorie sono della stessa invenzione, benchè di grandezze diverse"; Baldinucci 1974–75, 5: 347.

13 Fletcher 1979; L. Borean in Borean and Mason 2007, 264–65. The Frick painting was never recorded as part of Del Sera's collection.

14 Florence 1978–79; Conticelli and Sframeli 2017.

15 Baldassari 2015, 154–57, nos. 58–60.

16 Baldassari (2015, 154–57, no. 58) believes Del Sera's version to be that now in Birmingham. But the latter also included a portrait of Raffaello Ximenes as an armored soldier, which, in Baldinucci's account, seems to have appeared only in the version for Carlo Corbinelli (Baldinucci 1974–75, 5: 347).

17 Nethersole 2017–18, 48.

18 Del Bravo 1967. The drawing is stylistically very close to Dolci's copy after Michelangelo's portrait of Andrea Quaratesi; S. Bellesi in Florence 2015, 174, no. 8. It is catalogued in Stancari 2015–16, 97.

19 Anderson 1994.

20 Maidstone, Kent Archive Office, file U855 (E16 for the family descent).

21 Lord Bexley's will, stipulating that his cousin Arthur would inherit Foot's Cray, is referenced in Fisher 2009, 7: *sub voce* "Vansittart, Nicholas."

22 Pisa, Scuola Normale Superiore, Archivio Salviati (cited hereafter as ASP): I, filza 222, fasc. 30. On the history of the villa, see Guerrieri 2018, 20.

23 Sotheby's, London, July 9, 2019 (lot 107). Costner was paid for eight canvases representing as many Salviati estates, including "Ponte alla Badia": the canvases were 1½ *braccia* wide, that is, little more than 87 cm (Lusoli 2013, 1: 265–66). This is the exact measurement of the canvas sold at Sotheby's. The canvas was later included in an inventory of 1789 (Lusoli 2013, 2: 378).

24 Sotheby's, London, July 9, 2019 (lot 108). The portrait was listed in an inventory of 1697 at Villa Salviati at Ponte alla Badia (Lusoli 2013, 2: 343).

25 Christie's, London, December 8, 2009 (lot 26); the portrait at the Art Institute in Chicago is inv. 1960.1 and lot no. 237 at the "Bexley" sale. This same portrait is probably the "signora figura intiera con un crocifisso" inventoried in 1789 at Villa Salviati at Ponte alla Badia (Lusoli 2013, 2: 378).

26 Guerrieri 2018, 20.

27 On the history of the Vansittart family at this juncture, see Pine 1972, 279–81.

28 P. Perrin in San Francisco and Paris 2019–20, 70–75, no. 39. This may explain why a label on the back of the Frick portrait, probably transferred onto the new stretcher after 1906, reads, in French: "Le Titien N° 11193 / Portrait de Laurent de Medicis." To the left on the bare wood is stenciled the number "99 CG" in black.

29 Pender was a Scottish submarine communications cable pioneer; Ash 2018 (with much information on his twenty-one-year lease of Foot's Cray).

30 Most Salviati inventories are in ASP, I, filze 120–21 and 150 (many of which are transcribed in Lusoli 2013,

2: 279–384). See also Della Pergola 1960; Costamagna 2000. On the complex history of the Salviati collection between Rome and Florence, see Lusoli 2013, 1: 248–56.

31 "Il Signor Marchese mi ha sempre protetto e favorito in tutte le cose come sua creatura"; Florence, Archivio di Stato, Mediceo 1476, fasc. 1, c. 384. I would like to thank Maria Stella Alfonsi for this reference. On Paolo del Sera in Florence, see Alfonsi 2019.

32 Hurtubise 1985, 420–25, 491–93.

33 Christie, Manson & Woods, London, May 1–4, 1876, lot 204 (May 2). The sale was set up "pursuant to an order made on the 15th of March, 1876, in the Chancery Division of the High Court of Justice, by Vice-Chancellor Malins, in the suit of Vansittart v. Vansittart," a lawsuit between Coleraine R. Vansittart (plaintiff), his nephew Robert Arnold Vansittart (1851–1928), his uncle William Vansittart (1813–1876), and his distant cousin Edward Vansittart-Neale (1810–1892); cf. Kew, The National Archives, C 16/1044/U/V7A. The presence of the painting in two different auctions the same year must have been the origin of the confusion in Brockwell 1914b.

34 Graves 1970, 3: 212 (as confirmed by the annotated copy of the catalogue at the National Art Library, London). The role of Waters in the London art world of the 1870s warrants further study; cf. how many times his name comes up in Redford 1888, vol. 2.

35 Christie, Manson & Woods, London, June 24, 1876 (lot 122). An annotated copy of the auction catalogue at the library of the Clark Institute in Williamstown indicates that the painting sold for £95 and 11 shillings (not £96 and 11 shillings).

36 For the Edgell family, see Fox-Davies 1905, 430.

37 Christie's, London, May 12, 1906 (lot 75). Discussions in *Times* 1906, 7; *Art Journal* 1906a, 208–9; *Art Journal* 1906b. O'Neill (2018, 170) infers that the painting was then bought by Lord Grimthorpe, who put it on sale in 1906. Although there is no reference in the text, this information comes from *Art Journal* 1906a, 208–9. In fact, this latter source clarifies that the portrait by Titian that had recently been auctioned came "from another source" than Lord Grimthorpe and that, previously, "in 1876, coming from Foot's Cray Place, it [had] made 91 gs [*corr.* pounds] at Christie's."

38 An annotated copy in the library of the Warburg Institute in London includes the price (different from that stated in *The Times* [1906, 7], probably because it includes fees). According to Reitlinger (1961–70, 1: 466), the painting sold for £2,170.

39 O'Neill 2018, 185.

40 Bernard Berenson and Roger Fry were granted private access to the canvas, which was displayed at the National Gallery of Ireland by January 1908 and lent to an exhibition at the Grafton Galleries (London, 1909–10), after which it was reproduced in color in the *Medici Print Series*; O'Neill 2018, 170. Lane also managed to garner a mention by Ricketts (1910, 46), who explicitly wrote: "When I saw it again, the scales fell from my eyes." At this time, the painting was still eliciting excoriating comments; Holmes 1909, 73 ("a sort of generalisation of Titian's qualities"); Fry 1910 ("un certo fare giorgionesco" but "non ci sembra abbastanza forte per Tiziano").

41 *Times* 1911, 8.

42 In 1912, for instance, Lane offered to Frick the so-called "Demidoff Rembrandt"; O'Neill 2018, 172.

43 O'Neill 2018, 181. On Roehampton House, see Weedon et al. 1996, 47–53.

44 Christie's, London, June 26, 1914 (lot 66). The annotated copy of the auction catalogue at the Warburg Institute in London bears the price *13.000*, as in Brockwell 1914a, 5. Reitlinger (1961–70, 1: 466) gives a slightly different price (£13,650).

45 All the following information is in New York, The Frick Collection–Frick Art Reference Library Archives (cited hereafter as FARL), Art Collecting Files of Henry Clay Frick, Series I: Purchases (Container ID 3107300004004); combined with CF, 1915.1.116, Correspondence. The same documents are the basis for the shorter account of the purchase in Salzman 2008, 247–50 (see also 233–37); O'Neill 2018, 181–85.

46 Creelman would also be instrumental in selling to Frick Whistler's *Frances Leyland* (1916.1.133) and Van Dyck's *Sir John Suckling* (1918.1.44).

47 Bernard Berenson had cabled Duveen in May: "If Frick does not want to keep it, I would strongly urge you to take it for yourselves, if, as you tell me, he paid relatively little for it." Curious about the price, he asked: "was it under £10,000?"; Salzman 2008, 248. Against this backdrop, it seems unlikely that Frick was personally attached to the painting as a symbol of Masonic affiliation (as in Frick Symington Sanger 1998, 357).

48 O'Neill 2018, 198. The "insurance covering everything" for Titian's portrait cost $14.62.

49 Fischel 1924 ("zu weichlich auch für den jungen Tizian"); Heinemann 1928, 64 ("möchte ich die endgültige Entscheidung der Autorschaft offenlassen"); Berenson 1932, 573 (Titian); Suida 1933, 34 (Titian); Venturi 1933, pl. 511 (Titian); Phillips 1937, 69, 158 (Titian); Richter 1937, 230 ("Giorgionesque"); Morassi 1942 (Titian); Longhi 1978, 58 (Titian); Tietze 1950 (omitted, hence excluded from Titian's catalogue). Doubts about the attribution had been raised before, for instance in Holmes 1909, 73; Sketchley 1909, 363; Von Beckerath 1910, 278; Fry 1910, 36–37.

50 Frick wrote to De Wild in March 1918 about a previous discussion—"your argument convinced me you were right"—but asked De Wild to write more fully on the matter. A letter dated April 4, 1918, indicates that he received De Wild's written report, but the report does not survive in the archives; FARL, Henry Clay Frick Papers, Series: Letterpress Copybooks, vol. 40, cc. 332 and 344.

51 FARL, Henry Clay Frick Estate Inventory, 1920, with annotations and added pages, 1931–36.

52 Dell'Acqua 1955, 110, no. 27; Valcanover 1960, 1: 56; Berenson 1957, 189. Exceptions still in Trevisan 1950, 377 (a self-portrait by Giorgione); Coletti 1955, 62.

53 Examples go from Ricketts 1910, 46, to Garton 2009–10, 201.

54 A new date of birth for Giorgione, based on documentary evidence, is proposed in Anderson 2019.

55 The most lucid account of Giorgione's work (and myth) is Hope 2003 (and 2009–10). See also Facchinetti and Galansino 2016.

56 Cf. Hirst (1981, 92), who at the same time urges caution in "claims of absolute novelty," because much evidence has been lost.

57 "Quando vuoi ritrarre uno, ritrailo a cattivo tempo, sul far della sera, facendo stare il ritratto con la schiena accosto a uno de' muri di essa corte. Pon mente per le strade sul fare della sera ai visi di uomini e di donne, quando è cattivo tempo, quanta grazia e dolcezza si vede in essi"; Leonardo da Vinci 2019, 117.

58 "[Giorgione] attese al disegno e lo gustò grandemente, e in quello la natura lo favorì sì forte, che egli, innamoratosi delle cose belle di lei . . . tanto andò imitandola, che non solo egli acquistò nome d'aver passato Gentile e Giovanni Bellini, ma di competere con coloro che lavoravano in Toscana et erano autori della maniera moderna. Aveva veduto Giorgione alcune cose di mano di Lionardo, molto fumeggiate e cacciate, come si è detto, terribilmente di scuro: e questa maniera gli piacque tanto che mentre visse sempre andò dietro a quella, e nel colorito a olio la imitò grandemente"; Vasari 1966–87, 4 (text): 42. On the word "fumeggiate," see Hope 2009–10, 186.

59 "Tiziano dunque, veduto il fare e la maniera di Giorgione, lasciò la maniera di Giambellino, ancorché vi avesse molto tempo consumato, e si accostò a quella, così bene imitando in brieve tempo le cose di lui, che furono le sue pitture talvolta scambiate e credute opere di Giorgione. . . . A principio, dunque, che cominciò a seguitare la maniera di Giorgione, non avendo più che diciotto anni, fece il ritratto d'un gentiluomo da Ca' Barbarigo, amico suo"; Vasari 1966–87, 6 (text): 156.

60 The best analysis of the iconography is Nova 2008.

61 For an overview, see Nepi Sciré 1992. The far-from-direct impact of Leonardo is best accounted for in Holberton 2008.

62 See Aikema 2003–4.

63 Jewitt 2021, 202 (however, there is no reason not to attribute the landscape of the *Flight into Egypt* to Titian; I. Artemieva in Venice 2012, 72–77).

64 "E certo si può attribuire a miracolo che Tiziano, senza aver veduto alora le anticaglie di Roma, che furono lume a tutti i pittori eccellenti, solamente con quella poca favilluccia ch'egli aveva scoperta nelle cose di Giorgione, vide e conobbe l'idea del dipingere perfettamente"; Dolce 2000, 188.

65 On Vasari and Dolce, see Agosti 2013, 97, 103n.418.

66 For Vasari and Giorgione, see mainly Hope 2008, with important corrections in Agosti 2013, 109–13.

67 Vasari 1966–87, 7: 308; Hope 2008, 30–31. Although Agosti (2013, 109–13) has shown that Giorgione's life in the second edition was not printed prior to Vasari's travel to Venice in 1566, the substantial inconsistencies between the Giorgione of the life of Titian and the Giorgione of his own life seem to suggest that Giorgione's life of 1568 could have been modified only to a limited extent after the trip to Venice.

68 Haskell 1981, 590. The fact that on the back of the *Laura* Vincenzo Catena is identified as Giorgione's "colleague" further strengthens this doubt; see Waldeck 2016.

69 Nichols 2020, 200–202.

70 On Giorgione's patrons and collectors, see Settis 1981; Padoan 1981. See also Mason 2003–4; Lauber 2009–10.

71 Mazzotta 2012 (with Fredericksen 2013).

72 The importance of this episode is best analyzed in Romano 1981.

73 Brown 1982, 51, doc. 29.

74 "Le figure de li omini abbiano atto proprio alla loro operazione in modo che, vedendoli, tu intendi quel che per loro si pensi o dica; li quali saranno bene imparati [da] chi imiterà li moti delli muti, li quali parlano co' movimenti delle mani e degli occhi e ciglia e di tutta la persona nel voler isprimere il concetto de l'animo loro"; Leonardo da Vinci 2019, 108.

75 Among which should also be mentioned the advent of plate-glass, which "allowed painters, and their sitters, to rehearse in front of mirrors, to dramatize their own appearance"; Hills 1999, 186.

76 Bolzoni 2008, 2010.

77 See Gilbert 1973; Nichols 2013, 88.

78 Shearman 1992, 143–46. But see also Craven 1939, 70: "Everything that is tawdry or bourgeois has been omitted; he is a lord, or at least he satisfies the romantic conception of a lord, and has the dignity and the commanding touch of melancholy with which Titian adorned manly heroes. His identity is of no importance, his occupation irrelevant. He is a member of Titian's gallery of portraits which embody the aristocratic complacency of Venice."

79 See Bolzoni 2016 (with bibliography).

80 Ballarin 1983. The presence of a line from *Gli Asolani* in a portrait now in Parma (Complesso Monumentale della Pilotta, inv. GN309) strengthens this point.

81 See, in particular, Campbell 2013; but also see Gentili 2005, 50.

82 "Voglio io sia lo aspetto del nostro Cortegiano, non così molle et feminile, come si sforzano d'haver molti, che non solamente si crespano i capegli et spelano le ciglia, ma si strisciano con tutti que' modi che si faccian le più lascive et dishoneste femine del mondo; et pare che nello andare, nello stare et in ogni altro lor atto siano tanto teneri, et languidi, che le membra siano per staccarsi loro l'uno dall'altro; et pronuntiano quelle parole così afflitte, che in quel punto par che llospirito loro finisca"; Castiglione 2016, 2: 54.

83 "Nessun vago giovane veggo per via piè innanzi piè solo et pensoso portare se stesso, che io non istimi: 'Forse pensa costui hora della sua donna'"; Bembo 1991, 170.

84 For a short history of editions of *Gli Asolani*, see E. Curti in Padua 2013, 142–44, no. 2.1. As they signed an oath constituting their "Compagnia degli Amici" (Fellowship of Friends) about 1500, Bembo and his friends ruled that they would bind together their portraits in a book-like album with their faces on one side and their emblems on the other. This suggests that they had small portraits like Jacometto Veneziano's in mind (Mazzotta 2020, 25n.26) rather than Giorgione's.

85 Romani 2013, 45 (as foreshadowed in Dionisotti 1995, 119). Bembo used to call Bellini "il mio Bellin," which translates to "my Bellini" but also to "my little beauty." His contacts with intellectual circles are undeniable: Brown 2016; Mazzotta 2020, 19–42. Conversely, Padoan (1981) has argued convincingly against Giorgione as an intellectual painter, which is one of the disputable tenets of Ballarin (1979 and 1983).

86 Podro 1998, 91; Campbell 2013, 163.

87 In this respect, the Frick portrait is not too different from Pontormo's *Halberdier*, in which "arms and beauty are held in a similarly poignant, even provocative balance"—a painting that was on long-term loan to the Frick between 1970 and 1989 before being sold to the Getty Museum; Cropper 1997, 88–90.

88 Morassi 1954, 194 (before 1511); Pallucchini 1953, 101 (after 1515); Pallucchini 1958, 64, and Pallucchini 1965, no pagination (1515–20); Grier 1968, 2: 252 ("after 1515"); Pallucchini 1969, 262 (1516–18); Valcanover 1969, 98, no. 67 (ca. 1515); Wethey 1971, 149–50n.116 (ca. 1516); Hills 1999, 187 (ca. 1515); Valcanover 1999, 261 (ca. 1512); Pedrocco 2000, 95, no. 27 (ca. 1510/11); Joannides 2001, 100 ("surely of 1511, probably in the winter"); Brown 2006–7, 243 (1512–14); Humphrey 2007, 50–52 (1516); Philips 2008, 112 (1516); Garton 2009–10, 201 (1511–16); Joannides 2010, 51 (ca. 1511); Gentili 2012, 86 ("1515 o poco prima"); Nichols 2013, 89 (ca. 1516); Phillips 2008, 112–13 (1516); Ballarin 2016, 7: xxii–xxiii (ca. 1516).

89 Associations with *The Pastoral Concert*, for instance, in Morassi 1942, 180, and 1954, 194; Coletti 1955, 62; Joannides 2001, 100. The first association between the Frick and Städel portraits is in Meyer 1937, 306, followed by Pallucchini 1953, 101, and many others. The 1516-or-thereabouts dating had been proposed on other grounds by Suida (1933, 34).

90 On the painting, see Bardon 1995; more succinctly: A. Ballarin in Paris 1993, 340–48, no. 43.

91 Cf. Wilde 1974, 213–16: "It was only a small step to impart to a self-contained picture what had been achieved in the fresco figure [in Padua]."

92 "Kost 15 vngerisch duc[aten] Anno 1516": Sander 2004, 164–71; D. Bohde in Frankfurt 2019, 152–54, no. 51.

93 Daniela Bohde (in Frankfurt 2019, 152–54, no. 51) suggests that the Frankfurt painting dates from ca. 1510, moving the date of the Frick portrait to 1511.

94 Hope 2003, 38.

95 See, in particular, Cranston 2000, 37–44; Nieto Fernández 2017, 143–79.

96 Other examples may include the so-called *Schiavona* (inv. NG 5385) or the portrait on loan from Lord Halifax's collection (inv. L611), both at the National Gallery, London; see Wethey 1971, 139, no. 95; 149, no. 115.

97 The Frick Collection, Curatorial Department, Conservation Treatment Reports: no. 116, Titian, *Man in a Red Cap*, 1974. Somewhat incorrectly, Wethey (1971, 149–50, no. 116) understood that the parapet was "an addition."

98 The Frick Collection, Curatorial Department, Conservation Treatment Reports: no. 116, Titian, *Man in a Red Cap*, 1974. At the 1906 auction, the painting was 30½ by 25½ inches. Now, it measures 32⅜ × 28 in. (82.2 × 71.1 cm). The relining must have taken place very soon because the illustration in Arundel 1906 (pl. XVI) includes the "parapet." Significantly, no other illustrations published while the painting was in Lane's collection include the parapet; London 1909–10, no. 86; Sketchley 1909, 363; Fry 1910, 37; Ricketts 1910, pl. xxvii; *Connoisseur* 1911, 267. The painting had undergone other treatment at least in 1920 (?), 1923, 1933, 1935, 1938, 1964, 1974, 1983.

99 Other examples may include the so-called *Jacopo Sannazaro* at Hampton Court (inv. RCIN 407190), the so-called *Physician* at the Kunsthistorisches Museum, Vienna (inv. Gemäldegalerie, 94), and the *Gentleman in a Black Beret* (not Giovanni Bellini) at the Statens Museum for Kunst, Copenhagen (inv. DEP15), all of which, despite many attempts at different dating, are probably from the second half of the 1510s; see, respectively, Wethey 1971, 138, no. 93; 2: 121, no. 70; and 2: 105, no. 43. The Frick sitter can also be compared, in reverse, to the Virgin in the *Malchiostro Annunciation* in Treviso, which bears the date 1520, as ongoing restoration has now revealed.

100 Merckel (1980, 277) points out that a mosaic of the prophet Obadiah in the vault of the sacristy of St. Mark's Basilica seems a reversed image of the Frick portrait (Merckel 1994, 117, fig. 98, for an illustration). The mosaic was laid by Marco Luciano Rizzo, ca. 1524; Merckel 1996, 172.

101 Gronau 1904, 43.

102 L. Wolk-Simon in New York 2021, 110–12, no. 12. Joannides (2001, 212) sees the connection with Raphael's portrait but believes that Titian's predates it considerably.

103 See Menegatti 2002–7a and 2002–7b.

104 In this context, it should be added that in 1518 an unspecified pupil of Raphael's stayed in Ferrara on his way to buying colors in Venice; Ballarin 1985, 1: 78. Sodoma also likely traveled to Ferrara in the summer of 1518; Farinella 2014, 148–49.

105 Bodart 1998, 31, 186, doc. 1; Zeitz 2000, 16, 142, doc. 1.

106 M. Lucco in Ferrara, New York, and Los Angeles 1998, 235–36, no. 45; Pattanaro 2014, 208–9. Venturi (1933, pl. 51) referred to the Frick portrait as belonging to Titian's "Ferrarese period (1516–23)."

107 Importantly, in 1516, Ludovico Ariosto published in Ferrara the first edition of *Orlando Furioso* under the aegis of the Este household. Its relationship with Titian's portraiture has yet to be explored fully; Falomir 2016–17. The dialogue with Brescian portraiture at this point should not be disregarded; Passoni 2018 (where the Frick portrait, however, is dated too early) but mostly Nova 2006.

108 I would like to thank Jane Bridgeman and Virginia Hill for their guidance in identifying the clothing of the figure. The lynx fur is from a rather pale specimen or from a snow leopard (although this is less likely because the latter is even less easily attained); this subject is discussed in a letter of 1974 from H. B. House, curator at the New York Zoological Society; CF, 1915.1.116, Correspondence. Quondam (2007, 128) insists on the significance of wearing black. On vests lined in lynx fur, see Levi Pisetzky 1966, 151–52.

109 Welch 2009, 260–61: leather gloves such as these were slashed "as a sign of fashionable insouciance."

110 I am grateful to Pierre Terjanian and Mario Scalini for their help with the identification of the sword. On rapiers, see Norman 1980.

111 "'In questo veggiamo infinite varietà: et chi si veste alla franzese, chi alla spagnola, chi vol parer tedesco; né ci mancano anchor di quelli che si vestono alla foggia de' Turchi; chi porta la barba, chi no. Sarà adunque ben fatto saper in questa confusione elegere il meglio.' Disse Messer Federico: 'Io in vero non saprei dar regula determinata circa il vestire, se non che l'huom s'accommodasse alla consuetudine de i più: et poi che

(come voi dite) questa consuetudine è tanto varia, et che gl'Italiani tanto son vaghi d'abigliarsi alle altrui foggie, credo che ad ogn'uno sia licito vestirsi a modo suo'"; Castiglione 2016, 2: 164. Titian's *Ippolito de' Medici* at Palazzo Pitti (inv. Palatina 1912, no. 201) is a manifestation of this tendency.

112 Koos 2006, 278–79. Sixteenth-century inventories describe Lorenzo de' Medici's portrait by Raphael (fig. 20) as showing him dressed "in the French style"; Jones and Penny 1983, 163.

113 Pagnotta 1997, 232–35, no. 31.

114 J. O. Hand in Washington and Tallinn 2018, 78–82, no. 13.

115 The heraldry of the portrait does not match precisely that of the Trivulzio family; Passoni 2013, 160–65 (with bibliography); Viganò 2013, 134–37. It is worth noting that the transcription of "2" as "Z" is attested by contemporary epigraphy. See, for instance, the date of Gaudenzio Ferrari's polyptych at Arona.

116 Only Pallucchini (1965, no pagination) seems to call the sitter "giovane ufficiale."

117 Carriers of swords in portraits by Titian include Holy Roman emperors Charles V and Ferdinand I (the latter known only through copies); Philip II, King of Spain; Francis I, King of France; Pedro Álvarez de Toledo y Zúñiga, Viceroy of Naples; Johann Friedrich I, Elector of Saxony; Pierluigi and Ranuccio Farnese (and an unknown family member whose portrait is in Pommersfelden, catalogued by Wethey 1971, 99, no. 32: likely Ottavio, who also appears with a sword in *Paul III and His Nephews* at Capodimonte); Federico II Gonzaga, Marquess (later Duke) of Mantua; Francesco Maria I and Guidobaldo II della Rovere, dukes of Urbino; Alfonso I d'Este, Duke of Ferrara; Ippolito de' Medici; and military men of unmatched prestige, such as Gabriele Tadino, Alfonso d'Avalos, and Giovan Francesco Acquaviva d'Aragona or Gabriele Serbelloni (see Wethey 1980; Ost 1982). Four or five portraits by Titian with sitters carrying a sword have not been identified with certainty: the first, at the Alte Pinakothek (inv. 517), with an (autograph?) copy in Bitonto (Apulia), has been discussed as a portrait of a member of the Gonzaga family (A. Donati in Bitonto 2012–13, 312–15, no. 23); the second, a portrait at the Armand Hammer Collection, Los Angeles (AH90.77), often identified as Ferrante Gonzaga (M. Costantini in Paris 2006–7, 128, no. 24); the third and fourth, two portraits usually identified as members of the Corner family (Knox Averett 2011; Joannides 2013), who may have enjoyed a particular status as émigrés and family members of the queen of Cyprus. The three exceptions to the rule seem to be the late portraits of Antonio Porcia (Milan, Pinacoteca di Brera, inv. 5958), which appear to demonstrate Lomazzo's point (see note 119), Jacopo Strada (Vienna, Kunsthistorisches Museum, inv. Gemäldegalerie, 81), and possibly Agostino Landi, Count of Compiano and Bardi (Boston, Museum of Fine Arts, 43.83); on which see a forthcoming article by Giulia Zaccariotto.

118 See Sanudo 1980, 260–61.

119 "I mercanti e banchieri che non mai videro spada ignuda, a quali propriamente si aspetta la penna nell'orecchia con la gonella intorno et il giornale davanti, si ritraggono armati con bastoni in mano da generali, cosa veramente ridicola"; Lomazzo 1973–75, 2: 377.

120 Cf. also Guazzo 1993, 1: 140: "Ma è ben tanto maggiore l'indiscretezza d'alcuni ignobili ricchi i quali non si vergognano di vestirsi nobilmente e portare armi indorate a canto, con quegli altri ornamenti che converrebbono a' soli cavalieri. . . . Ed è scorsa ormai tanto oltre questa licenza in molte parti d'Italia . . . che non si conosce più alcuna distinzione de' gradi loro."

121 Morassi (1956, 127, and 1964, 18) identified the sitter as Giorgione (like Trevisan 1950, 377), who would also appear in a portrait by Titian in Petworth House (Wethey 1971, 104, no. 42)—an identification ruled out by color photography. David E. Squiers identified the sitter physiognomically, but questionably, with Charles of Bourbon; *Catalogue* 1949, 1: 258.

122 A good introduction to Federico's life is Benzoni 1995.

123 Cashman 2002. At court, he was invited to adopt French clothing and hairstyle; Welch 2009, 255–56.

124 See Barbieri 2011–12.

125 Cashman 2002, 342.

126 "El Signor [Federico] era ben in ordene, con uno sajon d'oro e bianco, et di sopra uno zupon di veluto negro e bareta di veluto in capo"; Sanuto 1889, 268. Also, "fo ordenato . . . di alozarlo in la casa fo dil marchese di Ferara" (*ivi*, 227): because the Gonzagas did not own a palazzo in Venice, Federico stayed there. In 1509, the republic took possession of the Fondaco de' Turchi from Federico's uncle Alfonso, assigning it to Pope Julius II in 1512. Leo X would then assign it to Altobello Averoldi in 1520, another patron of Titian's; it was only given back to Alfonso in 1531; Schulz 2004, 136–37.

127 Levi Pisetzky 1966, 157; Welch 2005, 267–70.

128 On this category, see Jenkins 1947; Oberhuber 1971.

129 Welch 2009, 255–56.

130 Isabella complained that her child's hair was too blond in the painting: A. Bayer in Berlin and New York 2011–12, 241–44, no. 93.

131 Ballarin 2002–7, 1: 328; Menegatti 2002–7c, 21–24.

132 See also Crowe and Cavalcaselle 1877, 1: 279–80.

133 "À veduto le cosse del Mantegna . . . e li à laudati li vostri studii"; Bodart 1998, 186, doc. 1.

134 "Volemo anche tu inviti maestro Tutiano pittor a venire a stare con noi queste feste presenti otto o diece giorni, pregandolo in nome nostro di ciò, ché l'haveremo molto grato et vederemolo volentieri"; Bodart 1998, 187, doc. 2.

135 The fact that Giambattista Malatesta started a letter of 1523 to Federico by saying, "El lator presente è maestro Ticiano," followed by all sorts of praise, does not necessarily mean he was introducing Titian *for the first time* to the marquess: one month later, Federico wrote to his uncle Alfonso, "Tyciano exhibitor presente" (Bodart 1998, 188, docs. 4–5), showing that this was simply a formula used to make sure that the letter was being delivered by its intended carrier. Though chronologically unreliable, it is also worth remembering Vasari's phrasing about the beginning of Titian's relationship with Federico: "*col quale* [Federico Gonzaga] *andato Tiziano al suo stato*, lo ritrasse che par vivo"; Vasari 1966–87, 6 (text): 162.

136 In April 1529, Titian was painting a portrait of Federico; Bodart 1998, 202–3, doc. 29. If it is the same that was seen in February 1530 by Giambattista Malatesta, it was "armato" and near to completion; Bodart 1998, 207, doc. 39. This is usually connected to a fragment in the collection of the dukes of Alba; Wethey 1971, 108, no. 49. However, after cleaning, the latter has emerged to be in fact a copy after Titian's *Francesco Maria I della Rovere* (I am grateful to Álvaro Romero Sanchez-Arjona for showing me the painting after restoration). No other copy after the portrait of Federico "armato" survives. It is unclear if this martial portrait was the one "che fece Messer Ticiano," chosen in 1531 to decorate the apartments of Margherita Paleologa (Luzio 1913, 29), or if the portrait for Margherita was the one at the Prado. The latter is sometimes identified with a "portrait" mentioned in the Gonzaga correspondence of 1523 (Bodart 1998, 192, doc. 11), for which alternative identifications abound; Bodart 1998, 35–40. Only two portraits of Federico were recorded in the far-from-complete inventories of the household at his death (1540): one "in etate giovanile," another "quadro grande cornisato de noce" (Ferrari 2003, 313–14, nos. 6648, 6661). They seem to survive in the inventories of 1626–27, where the latter is assigned to Titian; Morselli 2000, 289–90, nos. 914, 940. The former is likely a portrait commissioned from Raphael in 1513 and received in 1521; Shearman 2003, 1: 930. A portrait of Federico by Titian was sent to Ottheinrich von Wittelsbach, Elector Palatine, in December 1540; Bodart 1998, 162–65, 334–35, doc. 315. It is now identified with a portrait in a private collection; A. H. De Groft in Paris 2006–7, 126, no. 23. In fact, an identical portrait must have stayed in Mantua for a long time, for it was copied numerous times in the sixteenth and seventeenth centuries. Perhaps Ottheinrich was sent a copy or a second version of the portrait (the Gonzagas often asked Titian to paint multiple copies of the same portraits; Bodart 1998, 118–19). In 1573, Gasparo Visconti offered to help Duke Guglielmo Gonzaga by asking Wilhelm von Wittelsbach (not yet Duke) for the portrait of Federico II Gonzaga by Titian, which, after Ottheinrich's death, had apparently passed to the branch of the dukes of Bavaria. It is unknown if the request to Wittelsbach was made; Piccinelli 2003, 79–80, doc. 55. In any case, the portrait by Titian in the Gonzaga collection in 1540 and 1626–27 is unlikely to be the Prado portrait, which only reappeared in Spain in 1642; Lapenta and Morselli 2006, 243. Ultimately, no existing portrait of Federico by Titian can be linked securely to documentation. No elements whatsoever support the identification of the sitter in a portrait in the Koelliker collection in Milan (inv. LK0180) as Federico, despite many such attempts; cf. S. Saponaro in San Secondo di Pinerolo 2013, 52–57, with bibliography.

137 Bodart 1998, 17; R. Morselli in Lapenta and Morselli 2006, 108–13 (but cf. J. Habert in Paris 1993, 372–74, nos. 54–55).

138 Rubin 2007, 7.

139 Kossoff had formerly interned at The Frick Collection and was then studying with Anthony Blunt and Johannes Wilde at the Courtauld Institute of Art in London, about which she wrote amusing letters to Biebel; CF, 1915.1.116, Correspondence.

140 Cropper 1976 and 1986.

141 On the portrait, its history and interpretation, see Venice 2013–14.

142 This had many consequences for poems addressed to men by both men and women; Romei 2010.
143 A possibile exception may be Giovanni Antonio Boltraffio; Pederson 2014.
144 See Luchs 1995, in particular 3–5.
145 Cropper 1995. Contrary views in Campbell 2005.
146 See Rubin 2018.
147 "[Si vuol ben] fare i contorni di modo dolci, et sfumati, che ancho s'intenda quel che non si vedi, anzi che l'occhio pensi di vedere quello ch'egli non vede, che è un fuggir dolcissimo, una tenerezza nell'orizonte della vista nostra, che è, et non è, et che solo si fa con infinita pratica"; Barbaro 1987, 321. On this passage, see Koos 2006, 315–16n.464 (with bibliography).
148 As pointed out in Hills 1999, 188.
149 See Koos 2006, 277–94 (the best analysis of the painting to date); Koep 2017, 110–13. Against scruples about the proximity of a sitter who makes the viewer feel that they "ought not to be present"; Shearman 1992, 131.
150 Koos 2006, 285; Nichols 2013, 88.
151 Greer 1987, 187. See also Greer 2003, 22–24.
152 Podro 1998, 89.
153 On presence, portraiture, and friendship, see Cranston 2000, 62–97. My scholarship here is also indebted to Joanna Woodall's professorial lecture "Only Connect" delivered in February 2019 at the Courtauld Institute of Art in London.
154 Hazlitt 1844, 155.

BIBLIOGRAPHY

Agosti 2013 Agosti, Barbara. *Giorgio Vasari: Luoghi e tempi delle Vite*. Milan, 2013.

Ahearn 2003 Ahearn, Barry, ed. *The Correspondence of William Carlos Williams and Louis Zukofsky*. Middletown, CT, 2003.

Aikema 2003–4 Aikema, Bernard. "Giorgione: i rapporti con il nord e una nuova lettura della *Vecchia* e della *Tempesta*." In *Giorgione: "le maraviglie dell'arte,"* edited by Giovanna Nepi Scirè, 73–89. Exh. cat. Venice (Gallerie dell'Accademia), 2003–4.

Alfonsi 2019 Alfonsi, Maria Stella. "Da Venezia a Firenze, da fratello a fratello: note su alcuni passaggi di proprietà fra Paolo del Sera, Giovan Carlo e Leopoldo de' Medici." *Studi di storia dell'arte* 30 (2019): 273–310.

Anderson 1994 Anderson, Stanford. "Matthew Brettingham the Younger, Foots Cray Place, and the Secularization of Palladio's Villa Rotonda in England." *Journal of the Society of Architectural Historians* 53 (1994): 428–47.

Anderson 2019 Anderson, Jaynie. "Giorgione in Sydney." *Burlington Magazine* 161 (2019): 190–99.

***Art Journal* 1906a** "May in the Sale Rooms." *Art Journal* 39 (1906): 207–9.

***Art Journal* 1906b** "Art Sales of the Season." *Art Journal* 45 (1906): 301.

Ash 2018 Ash, Stewart. *The Cable King: The Life of John Pender*. Scotts Valley, CA, 2018.

Baldassari 2015 Baldassari, Francesca. *Carlo Dolci: Complete Catalogue of the Paintings*. Florence, 2015.

Baldinucci 1974–75 Baldinucci, Filippo. *Notizie dei professori di disegno da Cimabue in qua* [1681–1728]. Edited by Ferdinando Ranalli, with an apparatus by Paola Barocchi. 7 vols. Florence, 1974–75.

Ballarin 1979 Ballarin, Alessandro. "Una nuova prospettiva su Giorgione: la ritrattistica degli anni 1500–1503." In *Giorgione: Atti del convegno internazionale di studio per il 5° centenario della nascita*, edited by Rodolfo Pallucchini, 227–52. Castelfranco Veneto, 1979.

Ballarin 1983 Ballarin, Alessandro. "Giorgione e la compagnia degli amici: il 'Doppio ritratto' Ludovisi." In *Storia dell'arte italiana*, pt. 2, vol. 1, *Dal Medioevo al Quattrocento*, edited by Federico Zeri, 479–541. Turin, 1983.

Ballarin 1985 Ballarin, Alessandro. *Dosso Dossi: la pittura a Ferrara negli anni del ducato di Alfonso I*. 2 vols. Cittadella (Padua), 1985.

Ballarin 2002–7 Ballarin, Alessandro, ed. *Il camerino delle pitture di Alfonso I*. 6 vols. Cittadella (Padua), 2002–7.

Ballarin 2016 Ballarin, Alessandro. *Giorgione e l'umanesimo veneziano*. 7 vols. Verona, 2016.

Barbaro 1987 *Vitruvio: I dieci libri dell'architettura tradotti e commentati da Daniele Barbaro* [1567]. Edited by Manfredo Tafuri and Manuela Morresi. Milan, 1987.

Barbieri 2011–12 Barbieri, Nicoletta Ilaria. "Cultura letteraria attorno a Federico Gonzaga, primo Duca di Mantova." Ph.D. diss., Università Cattolica del Sacro Cuore, Milan, 2011–12.

Bardon 1995 Bardon, Françoise. *Le "Concert Champêtre."* 2 vols. Paris, 1995.

Bembo 1991 Bembo, Pietro. *Gli Asolani* [1505]. Edited by Giorgio Dilemmi. Florence, 1991.

Benzoni 1995 Benzoni, Gino. "Federico II Gonzaga, duca di Mantova e marchese del Monferrato." *Dizionario Biografico degli Italiani* 45 (1995): 710–22.

Berenson 1932 Berenson, Bernard. *Italian Pictures of the Renaissance: A List of the Principal Artists and Their Works.* Oxford, 1932.

Berenson 1957 Berenson, Bernard. *Italian Pictures of the Renaissance: A List of the Principal Artists and Their Works: Venetian School.* London, 1957.

Berlin and New York 2011–12 Keith Christiansen and Stefan Weppelmann, eds. *The Renaissance Portrait: From Donatello to Bellini.* Exh. cat. Berlin (Bode-Museum) and New York (Metropolitan Museum of Art), 2011–12.

Bitonto 2012–13 Nuccia Barbone Pugliese, Andrea Donati, and Lionello Puppi, eds. *Tiziano, Bordon e gli Acquaviva d'Aragona: pittori veneziani in Puglia e fuoriusciti napoletani in Francia.* Exh. cat. Bitonto (Galleria Nazionale della Puglia), 2012–13.

Bodart 1998 Bodart, Diane H. *Tiziano e Federico II Gonzaga: Storia di un rapporto di committenza.* Rome, 1998.

Bolzoni 2008 Bolzoni, Lina. *Poesia e ritratto nel Rinascimento.* Rome and Bari, 2008.

Bolzoni 2010 Bolzoni, Lina. *Il cuore di cristallo: Ragionamenti d'amore, poesia e ritratto nel Rinascimento.* Turin, 2010.

Bolzoni 2016 Bolzoni, Lina. "*Gli Asolani* e il fascino del ritratto." In *Pietro Bembo e le arti,* edited by Guido Beltramini, Howard Burns, and Davide Gasparotto, 285–308. Venice, 2016.

Borean and Mason 2007 Borean, Linda, and Stefania Mason, eds. *Il collezionismo d'arte a Venezia: Il Seicento.* Venice, 2007.

Brockwell 1914a [Brockwell, Maurice W.] "£106,000 Picture Sale / Dispersal of Mr Grenfell's Collection: The Titian Portrait." *The Times,* June 27, 1914.

Brockwell 1914b Brockwell, Maurice W. "Sir Hugh Lane's Titian." *The Times,* July 9, 1914.

Brown 1982 Brown, Clifford Malcolm. *Isabella d'Este and Lorenzo da Pavia: Documents for the History of Art and Culture in Renaissance Mantua.* Geneva, 1982.

Brown 2006–7 Brown, David Alan. "Portraits of Men." In *Bellini, Giorgione, Titian and the Renaissance of Venetian Painting,* edited by David Alan Brown et al., 237–45. Exh. cat. Washington (National Gallery of Art) and Vienna (Kunsthistorisches Museum), 2006–7.

Brown 2016 Brown, David Alan. "Bembo and Bellini." In *Pietro Bembo e le arti,* edited by Guido Beltramini, Howard Burns, and Davide Gasparotto, 309–27. Venice, 2016.

Campbell 2005 Campbell, Stephen J. "Eros in the Flesh: Petrarchan Desire, the Embodied Eros and Male Beauty in Italian Art, 1500–1540." *Journal of Medieval and Early Modern Studies* 35 (2005): 629–62.

Campbell 2013 Campbell, Stephen J. "Pietro Bembo e il ritratto del Rinascimento." In Padua 2013, 158–67.

Cashman 2002 Cashman, Anthony B., III. "Performing Anxiety: Federico Gonzaga at the Court of Francis I and the Uncertainty of Ritual Actions." *Sixteenth Century Journal* 33 (2002): 333–52.

Castiglione 2016 Castiglione, Baldassare. *Il Libro del Cortegiano* [1528]. Edited by Amedeo Quondam. 3 vols. Rome, 2016.

***Catalogue* 1949** *The Frick Collection: An Illustrated Catalogue of the Works of Art in the Collection of Henry Clay Frick*. 2 vols. Pittsburgh, 1949.

***Catalogue* 1968** *The Frick Collection: An Illustrated Catalogue. Paintings*. 2 vols. New York, 1968.

Coletti 1955 Coletti, Luigi. *Tutta la pittura di Giorgione*. Milan, 1955.

***Connoisseur* 1911** "Current Art Notes." *The Connoisseur: An Illustrated Magazine for Collectors* 115 (1911): 267–80.

***Connoisseur* 1914** "The Sale Room." *The Connoisseur: An Illustrated Magazine for Collectors* 156 (1914): 263–72.

Conticelli and Sframeli 2017 Conticelli, Valentina, and Maria Sframeli, eds. "Regesto dei dipinti." In *Leopoldo de' Medici, principe dei collezionisti*, edited by Valentina Conticelli, Riccardo Gennaioli, and Maria Sframeli, 531–65. Exh. cat. Florence (Gallerie degli Uffizi and Palazzo Pitti), 2017.

Costamagna 2000 Costamagna, Philippe. "La collection de peintures d'une famille florentine établie à Rome: l'inventaire après décès du duc Anton Maria Salviati dressé en 1704." *Nuovi studi* 5 (2000): 177–233.

Cranston 2000 Cranston, Jodi. *The Poetics of Portraiture in the Italian Renaissance*. Cambridge, England, 2000.

Craven 1939 Craven, Thomas, ed. *A Treasury of Art Masterpieces: From the Renaissance to the Present Day*. New York, 1939.

Cropper 1976 Cropper, Elizabeth. "On Beautiful Women, Parmigianino, Petrarchismo, and the Vernacular Style." *Art Bulletin* 58 (1976): 374–94.

Cropper 1986 Cropper, Elizabeth. "The Beauty of Women: Problems in the Rhetoric of Renaissance Portraiture." In *Rewriting the Renaissance: The Discourses of Sexual Difference in Early Modern Europe*, edited by Margaret G. Ferguson, Maureen Quilligan, and Nancy J. Vickers, 175–90. Chicago and London, 1986.

Cropper 1995 Cropper, Elizabeth. "The Place of Beauty in the High Renaissance and Its Displacement in the History of Art." In *Place and Displacement in the Renaissance*, edited by Alvin Vos, 159–205. Binghamton, 1995.

Cropper 1997 Cropper, Elizabeth. *Pontormo: Portrait of a Halberdier*. Los Angeles, 1997.

Crowe and Cavalcaselle 1877 Crowe, Joseph Archer, and Giovanni Battista Cavalcaselle. *Titian: His Life and Times*. 2 vols. London, 1877.

Del Bravo 1967 Del Bravo, Carlo. "Una copia da Tiziano." *Arte veneta* 21 (1967): 223.

Dell'Acqua 1955 Dell'Acqua, Gian Alberto. *Tiziano*. Milan, 1955

Della Pergola 1960 Della Pergola, Paola. "Gli inventari Salviati." *Arte antica e moderna* 11 (1960): 193–200, 308–21.

Dionisotti 1995 Dionisotti, Carlo. "Tiziano e la letteratura" [1976]. In *Appunti su arte e lettere*, by Carlo Dionisotti. Milan, 1995.

Dolce 2000 Dolce, Lodovico. *Dialogo della pittura intitolato L'Aretino* [1557]. Edited by Mark W. Roskill. Toronto, Buffalo, and London, 2000.

Facchinetti and Galansino 2016 Facchinetti, Simone, and Arturo Galansino. "The Biography of a Myth." In *In the Age of Giorgione*, edited by Simone Facchinetti, Arturo Galansino, and Per Rumberg, 18–33. Exh. cat. London (Royal Academy of Arts), 2016.

Falomir 2016–17 Falomir, Miguel. "Ariosto e Tiziano." In *Orlando Furioso 500 anni: Cosa vedeva Ariosto quando chiudeva gli occhi*, edited by Guido Beltramini and Alfonso Tura, 236–41. Exh. cat. Ferrara (Palazzo dei Diamanti), 2016–17.

Ferrara, New York, and Los Angeles 1998 Peter Humphrey and Mauro Lucco. *Dosso Dossi: Pittore di corte a Ferrara nel Rinascimento*. Exh. cat. Ferrara (Civiche Gallerie d'Arte Moderna e Contemporanea), New York (Metropolitan Museum of Art), and Los Angeles (The J. Paul Getty Museum), 1998.

Ferrari 2003 Ferrari, Daniela. *Le collezioni Gonzaga: L'inventario dei beni del 1540–1542*. Cinisello Balsamo, 2003.

Fischel 1924 Fischel, Oskar. *Tizian: des Meisters Gemälde*. Stuttgart, Berlin, and Leipzig, 1924.

Fisher 2009 Fisher, David R., ed. *The House of Commons, 1820–1832*. 7 vols. Cambridge, England, 2009.

Fletcher 1979 Fletcher, Jennifer. "Marco Boschini and Paolo del Sera: Collectors and Connoisseurs of Venice." *Apollo* 110 (1979): 416–24.

Fletcher 2003 Fletcher, Jennifer. "Titian as a Painter of Portraits." In *Titian*, edited by David Jaffé, 29–42. New Haven and London, 2003.

Florence 1978–79 Grazia Agostini et al., eds. *Tiziano nelle gallerie fiorentine*. Exh. cat. Florence (Palazzo Pitti), 1978–79.

Florence 2015 Sandro Bellesi and Anna Bisceglia, eds. *Carlo Dolci 1616–1687*. Exh. cat. Florence (Palazzo Pitti), 2015.

Fox-Davies 1905 Fox-Davies, Arthur Charles. *Armorial Families: A Directory of Gentlemen of Coat-Armour*. London, 1905.

Frankfurt 2019 Bastian Eclercy, ed. *Tizian und die Renaissance in Venedig*. Exh. cat. Frankfurt (Städel Museum), 2019.

Fredericksen 2013 Fredericksen, Burton. "Titian's Barbarigo Portrait and Lord Darnley." *Burlington Magazine* 155 (2013): 16–18.

Frick Symington Sanger 1998 Frick Symington Sanger, Martha. *Henry Clay Frick: An Intimate Portrait*. New York, London, and Paris, 1998.

Fry 1910 Fry, Roger E. "La mostra di antichi dipinti alle 'Grafton Galleries' di Londra." *Rassegna d'arte* 10 (1910): 35–39.

Garton 2009–10 Garton, John. "Gentlemen of Fashion." In *Titian, Tintoretto, Veronese: Rivals in Renaissance Venice*, edited by Frederick Ilchman, 201–2. Exh. cat. Boston (Museum of Fine Arts) and Paris (Musée du Louvre), 2009–10.

Gentili 2005 Gentili, Augusto. "Il gesto, l'abito, il monaco." *Studi tizianeschi* 3 (2005): 46–56.

Gentili 2012 Gentili, Augusto. *Tiziano*. Milan, 2012.

Gilbert 1973 Gilbert, Felix. "Venice in the Crisis of the League of Cambrai." In *Renaissance Venice*, edited by John R. Hale, 274–92. London, 1973.

Graves 1970 Graves, Algernon. *Art Sales from Early in the Eighteenth Century to Early in the Twentieth Century (Mostly Old Masters and Early English Pictures)* [1918–21]. 3 vols. New York, 1970.

Greer 1987 Greer, Germaine. "What Turns Women On" [1973]. In *The Madwoman's Underclothes: Essays and Occasional Printings*, by Germaine Greer, 178–88. New York, 1987.

Greer 2003 Greer, Germaine. *The Boy*. London, 2003.

Gronau 1904 Gronau, Georg. *Titian*. London and New York, 1904.

Guazzo 1993 Guazzo, Stefano. *La civil conversazione* [1574]. Edited by Amedeo Quondam. 2 vols. Modena, 1993.

Guerrieri 2018 Guerrieri, Francesco. "Le coordinate storiche." In *Villa Salviati alla Badia: Il restauro*, edited by Francesco Guerrieri and Renzo Renai, 13–20. Florence, 2018.

Haskell 1981 Haskell, Francis. "La sfortuna critica di Giorgione." In *Giorgione e l'umanesimo veneziano*, vol. 2, edited by Rodolfo Pallucchini, 583–606. Florence, 1981.

Hazlitt 1844 Hazlitt, William. *Criticism on Art*. London, 1844.

Heinemann 1928 Heinemann, Fritz. *Tizian: Die zwei ersten Jahrzehnte seiner künstlerischen Entwicklung*. Munich, 1928.

Hills 1999 Hills, Paul. *Venetian Colour: Marble, Mosaic, Painting and Glass, 1250–1550*. New Haven and London, 1999.

Hirst 1981 Hirst, Michael. *Sebastiano del Piombo*. Oxford, 1981.

Holberton 2008 Holberton, Paul. "Giorgione's sfumato." In *Giorgione entmythisiert*, edited by Sylvia Ferino-Pagden, 55–69. Turnhout, 2008.

Holmes 1909 Holmes, Charles J. "'The School of Giorgione' at the Grafton Galleries." *Burlington Magazine for Connoisseurs* 16 (1909): 72–74.

Hope 2003 Hope, Charles. *Giorgione or Titian? History of a Controversy*. New York, 2003.

Hope 2008 Hope, Charles. "Giorgione in Vasari's *Vite*." In *Giorgione entmythisiert*, edited by Sylvia Ferino-Pagden, 15–37. Turnhout, 2008.

Hope 2009–10 Hope, Charles. "Giorgione nei documenti e nelle fonti." In *Giorgione*, edited by Enrico Maria dal Pozzolo and Lionello Puppi, 179–88. Exh. cat. Castelfranco Veneto (Museo Casa Giorgione), 2009–10.

Humphrey 2007 Humphrey, Peter. *Titian*. London, 2007.

Hurtubise 1985 Hurtubise, Pierre. *Une famille-témoin: les Salviati*. Vatican City, 1985.

Jenkins 1947 Jenkins, Marianna. *The State Portrait: Its Origins and Evolution*. New York, 1947.

Jewitt 2021 Jewitt, James R. "Revisiting Titian's 'Flight into Egypt' at Ca' Loredan, Venice." *Burlington Magazine* 163 (2021): 28–33.

Joannides 2001 Joannides, Paul. *Titian to 1518: The Assumption of Genius*. New Haven and London, 2001.

Joannides 2010 Joannides, Paul. "Le jeune Titien portraitiste." In *Titien, l'étrange homme au gant*, edited by Paul Joannides, 13–83. Exh. cat. Ajaccio (Palais Fesch), 2010.

Joannides 2013 Joannides, Paul. "A Portrait by Titian of Girolamo Cornaro." *Artibus et historiae* 67 (2013): 239–49.

Jones and Penny 1983 Jones, Roger, and Nicholas Penny. *Raphael*. New Haven and London, 1983.

Judd 2016 Judd, Donald. "New York City—A World Art Center" [1962]. In *Donald Judd Writings*, edited by Flavin Judd and Caitlin Murray, 72–81. New York, 2016.

Knox Averett 2011 Knox Averett, Matthew. "Becoming Giorgio Cornaro: Titian's 'Portrait of a Man with a Falcon.'" *Zeitschrift für Kunstgeschichte* 74 (2011): 559–68.

Koep 2017 Koep, Daniel. "Das Männerporträt zwischen Macht und Eros." In *Die Poesie der venezianischen Malerei: Paris Bordone, Palma il Vecchio, Lorenzo Lotto, Tizian*, edited by Sandra Pisot, 104–17. Hamburg, 2017.

Koos 2006 Koos, Marianne. *Bildnisse des Begehrens: Das lyrische Männerporträt in der venezianischen Malerei des frühen 16. Jahrhunderts—Giorgione, Tizian und ihr Umkreis*. Berlin, 2006.

Lapenta and Morselli 2006 Lapenta, Stefania, and Raffaella Morselli. *Le collezioni Gonzaga: La quadreria nell'elenco dei beni del 1626–1627*. Cinisello Balsamo, 2006.

Lauber 2009–10 Lauber, Rosella. "Una lucente linea d'ombra. Note per Giorgione nel collezionismo veneziano." In *Giorgione*, edited by Enrico Maria dal Pozzolo and Lionello Puppi, 189–206. Exh. cat. Castelfranco Veneto (Museo Casa Giorgione), 2009–10.

Leonardo da Vinci 2019 Leonardo da Vinci. *Libro di pittura* [before 1542]. Edited by Maria Teresa Fiorio. Milan, 2019.

Levi Pisetzky 1966 Levi Pisetzky, Rosita. *Storia del costume in Italia*. Vol. 3. Rome, 1966.

Lomazzo 1973–75 Lomazzo, Gian Paolo. *Scritti sulle arti* [1584]. Edited by Roberto Paolo Ciardi. 2 vols. Florence, 1973–75.

London 1909–10 Charles Holroyd, ed. *A Catalogue of the Pictures and Drawings in the National Loan Exhibition in Aid of National Gallery Funds*. Exh. cat. London (Grafton Galleries), 1909–10.

Longhi 1978 Longhi, Roberto. "Viatico per cinque secoli di pittura veneziana" [1945–46]. In *Opere complete di Roberto Longhi*, vol. 10, *Ricerche sulla pittura veneta (1946–1969)*, 1–63. Florence, 1978.

Lucco 1983 Lucco, Mauro. "Venezia fra Quattro e Cinquecento." In *Storia dell'arte italiana*, part 2, vol. 1, *Dal Medioevo al Quattrocento*, edited by Federico Zeri, 445–77. Turin, 1983.

Luchs 1995 Luchs, Alison. *Tullio Lombardo and Ideal Portrait Sculpture in Renaissance Venice, 1490–1530*. Cambridge, England, 1995.

Lusoli 2013 Lusoli, Monica. "Villa Salviati del Ponte alla Badia." 2 vols. Ph.D. diss., Università degli Studi di Firenze, Florence, 2013.

Luzio 1913 Luzio, Alessandro. *La galleria dei Gonzaga, venduta all'Inghilterra nel 1627–28*. Milan, 1913.

Mason 2003–4 Mason, Stefania. "'Di mano di questo maestro pochissime sono le cose che si vedono': Giorgione nel collezionismo veneziano." In *Giorgione: "Le maraviglie dell'arte,"* edited by Giovanna Nepi Scirè, 65–71. Exh. cat. Venice (Gallerie dell'Accademia), 2003–4.

Mazzotta 2012 Mazzotta, Antonio. "A 'Gentiluomo da Ca' Barbarigo' by Titian in the National Gallery, London." *Burlington Magazine* 154 (2012): 12–19.

Mazzotta 2020 Mazzotta, Antonio. *Con Giovanni Bellini: Dodici esercizi di lettura*. Rome, 2020.

Menegatti 2002–7a Menegatti, Maria Lucia. "Regesto degli artisti." In Ballarin 2002–7, 1: 403–63.

Menegatti 2002–7b Menegatti, Maria Lucia. "Documenti per la storia dei camerini di Alfonso I (1471–1643). Regesto generale." In Ballarin 2002–7, 3: 3–340.

Menegatti 2002–7c Menegatti, Maria Lucia. "Archivio di Stato di Mantova. Archivio Gonzaga: spigolature archivistiche (1505–1534)." In Ballarin 2002–7, 5: 5–41.

Merckel 1980 Merckel, Ettore. "Tiziano e i mosaicisti a San Marco." In *Tiziano e Venezia: Convegno internazionale di studi (Venezia, 1976)*, edited by Neri Pozza et al., 275–83. Venice, 1980.

Merckel 1994 Merckel, Ettore. "I mosaici del Cinquecento veneziano (I parte)." *Saggi e memorie di storia dell'arte* 19 (1994): 73–140.

Merckel 1996 Merckel, Ettore. "I mosaici del Cinquecento veneziano (II parte)." *Saggi e memorie di storia dell'arte* 20 (1996): 95–195.

Meyer 1937 Meyer, August L. "À propos d'un nouveau livre sur le Titien." *Gazette des Beaux-Arts* 18 (1937): 304–11.

Morassi 1942 Morassi, Antonio. *Giorgione*. Milan, 1942.

Morassi 1954 Morassi, Antonio. "Esordi di Tiziano." *Arte veneta* 8 (1954): 178–98.

Morassi 1956 Morassi, Antonio. "Ritratti del periodo giovanile di Tiziano." In *Festschrift W. Sas-Zaloziecky zum 60. Geburtstag*, edited by Gertrude Gsodam, 125–31. Graz, 1956.

Morassi 1964 Morassi, Antonio. *Tiziano*. Milan, 1964.

Morselli 2000 Morselli, Raffaella. *Le collezioni Gonzaga: L'elenco dei beni del 1626–1627*. Cinisello Balsamo, 2000.

Nepi Sciré 1992 Nepi Sciré, Giovanna. "Venezia e la pittura attorno al 1500." In *Leonardo & Venezia*, edited by Nepi Sciré and Pietro C. Marani, 65–84. Exh. cat. Venice (Palazzo Grassi), 1992.

Nethersole 2017–18 Nethersole, Scott. "Carlo Dolci and the Art of the Past." In *Carlo Dolci: The Medici's Painter and 17th-Century Florence*, edited by Eve Straussman-Pflanzer, 43–53. Exh. cat. Wellesley (Davis Museum at Wellesley College) and Durham (Nasher Museum of Art at Duke University), 2017–18.

New York 2021 Keith Christiansen and Carlo Falciani, eds. *The Medici: Portraits and Politics, 1512–1570*. Exh. cat. New York (Metropolitan Museum of Art), 2021.

Nichols 2013 Nichols, Tom. *Titian and the End of the Venetian Renaissance*. London, 2013.

Nichols 2020 Nichols, Tom. *Giorgione's Ambiguity*. London, 2020.

Nieto Fernández 2017 Nieto Fernández, Luis. *The Painted Parapet: Structure and Symbolism / El parapeto pintado: Estructura y simbolismo*. Madrid, 2017.

Norman 1980 Norman, Alexander Vesey Bethune. *The Rapier and the Small-Sword, 1460–1820*. London, 1980.

Nova 2006 Nova, Alessandro. "Centro, periferia, provincia." In *Romanino: Un pittore in rivolta nel Rinascimento italiano*, edited by Lia Camerlengo et al., 48–67. Exh. cat. Trent (Castello del Buonconsiglio), 2006.

Nova 2008 Nova, Alessandro. "Giorgione e Tiziano al Fondaco dei Tedeschi." In *Giorgione entmythisiert*, edited by Sylvia Ferino-Pagden, 71–104. Turnhout, 2008.

Oberhuber 1971 Oberhuber, Konrad. "Raphael and the State Portrait." *Burlington Magazine* 113 (1971): 124–31, 436–43.

O'Neill 2018 O'Neill, Morna. *Hugh Lane: The Art Market and the Art Museum, 1893–1915*. New Haven and London, 2018.

Ost 1982 Ost, Hans. *Tizians Kasseler Kavalier: Ein Beitrag zum höfischen Porträt unter Karl V.* Cologne, 1982.

Padoan 1981 Padoan, Giorgio. "Il mito di Giorgione intellettuale." In *Giorgione e l'umanesimo veneziano*, vol. 1, edited by Rodolfo Pallucchini, 425–55. Florence, 1981.

Padua 2013 Guido Beltramini, Davide Gasparotto, and Adolfo Tura, eds. *Pietro Bembo e l'invenzione del Rinascimento*. Exh. cat. Padua (Palazzo del Monte di Pietà), 2013.

Pagnotta 1997 Pagnotta, Laura. *Bartolomeo Veneto: L'opera completa*. Florence, 1997.

Pallucchini 1953 Pallucchini, Rodolfo. *Tiziano: Lezioni tenute alla Facoltà di Lettere dell'Università di Bologna durante l'anno 1952–53*. Edited by Ornella Fanti and Lidia Mandelli Puglioli. Bologna, 1953.

Pallucchini 1958 Pallucchini, Rodolfo. "Un nuovo ritratto di Tiziano." *Arte veneta* 12 (1958): 63–69.

Pallucchini 1965 Pallucchini, Rodolfo. *I maestri del colore: Tiziano*. Vol. 1. Milan, 1965.

Pallucchini 1969 Pallucchini, Rodolfo. *Tiziano*. Florence, 1969.

Paris 1993 Michel Laclotte and Giovanna Nepi Scirè, eds. *Le siècle de Titien: L'âge d'or de la peinture à Venise*. Exh. cat. Paris (Grand Palais), 1993.

Paris 2006–7 Patrizia Nitti, Tullia Carratù, and Morena Costantini, eds. *Titien: Le pouvoir en face*. Exh. cat. Paris (Musée du Luxembourg), 2006–7.

Passoni 2013 Passoni, Maria Chiara. "La ritrattistica di Bernardino de Conti: alcune precisazioni sulla committenza." In *Le Duché de Milan et les commanditaires français (1499–1521)*, edited by Frédéric Elsig and Mauro Natale, 145–79. Rome, 2013.

Passoni 2018 Passoni, Maria Chiara. "Circolazione di modelli tra Venezia e Brescia. Il ritratto." In *Tiziano e la pittura del Cinquecento tra Venezia e Brescia*, edited by Francesco Frangi, 142–47. Exh. cat. Brescia (Museo di Santa Giulia), 2018.

Pattanaro 2014 Pattanaro, Alessandra. "Ritratti di principi, condottieri, umanisti e cortigiani." In *Dosso Dossi: Rinascimenti eccentrici al Castello del Buonconsiglio*, edited by Vincenzo Farinella, 107–17. Exh. cat. Trent (Castello del Buonconsiglio), 2014.

Pederson 2014 Pederson, Jill. "Giovanni Antonio Boltraffio's Portrait of Girolamo Casio and the Poetics of Male Beauty in Renaissance Milan." In *Renaissance Love: Eros, Passion, and Friendship in Italian Art around 1500*, edited by Jeanette Kohl, Marianne Koos, and Adrian W. B. Randolph, 165–84. Berlin and Munich, 2014.

Pedrocco 2000 Pedrocco, Filippo. *Tiziano*. Milan, 2000.

Phillips 1937 Phillips, Duncan. *The Leadership of Giorgione*. Washington, DC, 1937.

Phillips 2008 Phillips, Claude. *Titian*. New York, 2008.

Piccinelli 2003 Piccinelli, Roberta. *Le collezioni Gonzaga: Il carteggio tra Milano e Mantova (1563–1634)*. Cinisello Balsamo, 2003.

Pine 1972 Pine, Leslie G. *The New Extinct Peerage 1884–1971: Containing Extinct, Abeyant, Dormant and Suspended Peerages with Genealogies and Arms*. London, 1972.

Podro 1998 Podro, Michael. *Depiction*. New Haven and London, 1998.

Quondam 2007 Quondam, Amedeo. *Tutti i colori del nero: Moda e cultura nell'Italia del Cinquecento*. Costabissara, 2007.

Redford 1888 Redford, George. *Art Sales: A History of Sales of Pictures and Other Works of Art*. 2 vols. London, 1888.

Reitlinger 1961–70 Reitlinger, Gerald. *The Economics of Taste*. 3 vols. London, 1961–70.

Richter 1937 Richter, George Martin. *Giorgio da Castelfranco, called Giorgione*. Chicago, 1937.

Ricketts 1910 Ricketts, Charles. *Titian*. London, 1910.

Romani 2013 Romani, Vittoria. "Pietro Bembo tra cultura figurativa cortigiana e 'maniera moderna.'" In *Pietro Bembo e l'invenzione del Rinascimento*, edited by Guido Beltramini, Davide Gasparotto, and Adolfo Tura, 32–47. Exh. cat. Padua (Palazzo del Monte di Pietà), 2013.

Romano 1981 Romano, Giovanni. "Verso la maniera moderna: da Mantegna a Raffaello." In *Storia dell'arte italiana*, pt. 2, vol. 2, *Dal Cinquecento all'Ottocento*, edited by Federico Zeri, 23–85. Turin, 1981.

Romei 2010 Romei, Danilo. "Saggi di poesia omoerotica volgare." In *Extravagances amoureuses: L'amour au-delà de la norme à la Renaissance / Stravaganze amorose: L'amore oltre la norma nel Rinascimento*, edited by Élise Boillet and Chiara Lastraioli, 235–62. Paris, 2010.

Rubin 2007 Rubin, Patricia Lee. *Portraits of the Artist as a Young Man: Parmigianino ca. 1524*. Groningen, 2007.

Rubin 2018 Rubin, Patricia Lee. *Seen from Behind: Perspectives on the Male Body and Renaissance Art*. New Haven and London, 2018.

Salzman 2008 Salzman, Cynthia. *Old Masters, New World: America's Raid on Europe's Great Pictures, 1880–World War I*. London, 2008.

Sander 2004 Sander, Jochen. *Italienische Gemälde im Städel 1300–1550: Oberitalien, die Marken und Rom*. Frankfurt, 2004.

San Francisco and Paris 2019–20 Marine Kisiel, Paul Perrin, and Cyrille Sciama, eds. *James Tissot: L'ambigu moderne*. Exh. cat. San Francisco (Fine Arts Museum, Legion of Honor) and Paris (Musée d'Orsay), 2019–20.

San Secondo di Pinerolo 2013 Vittorio Sgarbi, ed. *I volti e l'anima: Tiziano. Ritratti*. Exh. cat. San Secondo di Pinerolo (Castello di Miradolo), 2013.

Sanudo 1980 Sanudo, Marin, il giovane. *De origine, situ et magistratibus urbis Venetae; ovvero, La città di Venezia (1493–1530)*. Edited by Angela Caracciolo Aricò. Milan, 1980.

Sanuto 1889 Sanuto, Marino. *I Diarii*. Vol. 24 [March–September 1517]. Venice, 1889.

Schulz 2004 Schulz, Juergen. *The New Palaces of Medieval Venice*. University Park, PA, 2004.

Settis 1981 Settis, Salvatore. "Giorgione e i suoi committenti." In *Giorgione e l'umanesimo veneziano*, vol. 1, edited by Rodolfo Pallucchini, 373–98. Florence, 1981.

Shearman 1992 Shearman, John. *Only Connect. . . Art and the Spectator in the Italian Renaissance*. Washington and Princeton, 1992.

Shearman 2003 Shearman, John. *Raphael in Early Modern Sources (1483–1602)*. 2 vols. New Haven and London, 2003.

Sketchley 1909 Sketchley, R[ose] E[sther] D[orothea]. "The National Loan Exhibition." *Art Journal* 75 (1909): 359–64.

Stancari 2015–16 Stancari, Isabella. "Il fondo storico dei disegni di Tiziano al Gabinetto Disegni e Stampe delle Gallerie degli Uffizi: dalla classificazione inventariale alla critica moderna." M.A. thesis, Università degli Studi di Bologna, 2015–16.

Suida 1933 Suida, Wilhelm. *Tizian*. Zurich and Leipzig, 1933.

Tietze 1950 Tietze, Hans. *Titian: The Paintings and Drawings*. New York, 1950.

***Times* 1906** *The Times* (London), May 14, 1906.

***Times* 1911** *The Times* (London), March 6, 1911.

***Times* 1914** *The Times* (London), July 8, 1914.

Trevisan 1950 Trevisan, Luca Luciano. *Giorgione*. Vol. 1. Venice, 1950.

Valcanover 1960 Valcanover, Francesco. *Tutta la pittura di Tiziano*. 2 vols. Milan, 1960.

Valcanover 1969 Valcanover, Francesco. *L'opera completa di Tiziano*. Milan, 1969.

Valcanover 1999 Valcanover, Francesco. *Tiziano: I suoi pennelli sempre partorirono espressioni di vita*. Florence, 1999.

Vasari 1966–87 Vasari, Giorgio. *Le vite de' più eccellenti pittori, scultori e architettori (nelle redazioni del 1550 e 1568)*. Edited by Paola Barocchi and Rosanna Bettarini. 6 vols. Florence, 1966–87.

Venice 2012 Irina Artemieva and Giuseppe Pavanello, eds. *Tiziano: La Fuga in Egitto e la pittura di paesaggio*. Exh. cat. Venice (Gallerie dell'Accademia), 2012.

Venice 2013–14 Giulio Manieri Elia and Fausta Navarro, eds. *La Bella di Tiziano a Palazzo Grimani*. Exh. cat. Venice (Museo di Palazzo Grimani), 2013–14.

Venturi 1933 Venturi, Lionello. *Italian Paintings in America*. Vol. 3, *Sixteenth to Eighteenth Century*. New York and Milan, 1933.

Viganò 2013 Viganò, Marino. "Bramantino a Milano: precisazioni 'trivulziane.'" *Raccolta vinciana* 35 (2013): 117–52.

Von Beckerath 1910 Von Beckerath, Adolph. "Drei Winter-Ausstellungen alter Bilder in London." *Repertorium für Kunstwissenschaft* 33 (1910): 278–86.

Waldeck 2016 Waldeck, Anik. "Vincenzo Catena and Giorgione, Reconsidered." *Artibus et historiae* 37 (2016): 59–71.

Washington and Tallinn 2018 John Oliver Hand and Greta Koppel, eds. *Michael Sittow: Estonian Painter at the Courts of Renaissance Europe*. Exh. cat. Washington (National Gallery of Art) and Tallinn (Art Museum of Estonia), 2018.

Weedon et al. 1996 Weedon, Brenda, et al. *A History of Queen Mary University Hospital Roehampton*. Edited by Helen Alper. Richmond, Twickenham, and Roehampton, 1996.

Welch 2005 Welch, Evelyn. *Shopping in the Renaissance: Consumer Cultures in Italy 1400–1600*. New Haven and London, 2005.

Welch 2009 Welch, Evelyn. "Art on the Edge: Hair and Hands in Renaissance Italy." *Renaissance Studies* 23 (2009): 241–68.

Wethey 1971 Wethey, Harold E. *The Paintings of Titian*. Vol. 2, *The Portraits*. London, 1971.

Wethey 1980 Wethey, Alice S. "Two Portraits of Noblemen in Armor and Their Heraldry." *Art Bulletin* 62 (1980): 76–96.

Wilde 1974 Wilde, Johannes. *Venetian Art from Bellini to Titian*. Oxford, 1974.

Woodward 1963 Woodward, John. "Museum Acquisitions: Paintings by Dolci and Claude for Birmingham." *Apollo* 77 (1963): 250–52.

Zeitz 2000 Zeitz, Lisa. *"Tizian, teurer Freund. . .": Tizian und Federico Gonzaga. Kunstpatronage in Mantua im 16. Jahrhundert.* Petersberg, 2000.

INDEX

Page numbers in *italics* refer to illustrations.

IMAGE CREDITS

Photographs have been provided by the owners or custodians of the works. The following list applies to those photographs for which a separate credit is due.

Fig. 1. Photo Joseph Coscia Jr.

Fig. 4. Smith Archive / Alamy Stock Photo

Fig. 5. Courtesy Sotheby's, Inc. © Private Collection, 2019

Figs. 6, 16, 19, 23. © RMN-Grand Palais / Art Resource, NY

Fig. 8. Shawshots / Alamy Stock Photo / photo John S. Johnston

Fig. 13. © The State Hermitage Museum / photo Vladimir Terebenin

Fig. 14. National Trust Photo Library / Art Resource, NY

Fig. 15. © National Gallery, London / Art Resource, NY

Fig. 19. bpk Bildagentur / Art Resource, NY

Fig. 20. HIP / Art Resource, NY

Fig. 23. © The Museum of Fine Arts, Houston / photo Jud Haggard

Fig. 25. © Detroit Institute of Arts / Bridgeman Images

Fig. 26. © Museo Nacional del Prado / Art Resource, NY

Fig. 28. © The Metropolitan Museum of Art / Art Resource, NY

Fig. 30. KHM-Museumsverband